CHRISTMAS CRAFTS

CHRISTMAS CRAFTS

Things to make the 24 days before Christmas

by Carolyn Meyer

Pictures by Anita Lobel

Harper & Row, Publishers

New York, Evanston, San Francisco, London

CHRISTMAS CRAFTS: Things to make the 24 days before Christmas
Text copyright © 1974 by Carolyn Meyer
Illustrations copyright © 1974 by Anita Lobel
Library of Congress Catalog Card Number: 74–2608
Trade Standard Book Number: 06–024197–7
Harpercrest Standard Book Number: 06–024198–5
FIRST EDITION

For Doris Majer Springer

CONTENTS

INTRODUCTION

Nobody knows exactly when—what day, what month, or even what year—Christ was born. The earliest Christians paid no attention to the birth date of the man they believed was the Son of God. But later worshipers of Jesus wanted a special day to be set aside for the celebration of his birth.

After several different dates had been observed and changed, Pope Julius I decided in the year A.D. 350 to make December 25 the date of Christmas—"Christ's Mass." He had a very practical reason for selecting that date: It was the day celebrated as the "Birthday of the Unconquered Sun" by many non-Christian Romans who worshiped the Persian god Mithras. At the same time, many other Romans with different beliefs were celebrating the Saturnalia, in honor of the god of agriculture. And followers of other religions were honoring the return of the sun with midwinter festivities.

In those days many people worshiped the sun, which gave them light and warmth and helped them grow their food. For months the days became shorter, and less and less was seen of the sun. Watching it gradually seem to disappear was a frightening experience. Then, around December 22 when the days began to grow longer again, its return was a cause for celebration.

It seemed to the early Christians that a celebration of the birth of Christ fit in well with these pagan observances. Since the Christians were often persecuted for their beliefs, it was easier to go along with local customs than to attract attention by being different. Gradually the Christians also adopted not only the pagan date but also many of the pagan customs—such as having evergreens in the house, giving gifts to one another, and even kissing under the mistletoe.

As the centuries passed, the forms of celebration changed in some ways. For a while, in seventeenth-century England, Christmas was a time for raucous and sometimes mischievous merrymaking. When Oliver Cromwell's Puritan government took over in 1642, Christmas celebrations were outlawed, and anyone caught observing the day in even the most innocent way was punished. Then King Charles II came to the English throne and in 1660 the celebration of Christmas was restored to the English people.

In the American colonies settled by the Puritans, the ban lasted a much longer time. A law in New England in 1659 forbade all Christmas celebration. Even after the law was repealed in 1681, disapproval of merrymaking persisted in these colonies for more than a century.

Such a dreary outlook, fortunately, did not last forever. The joy of Christmas had spread throughout Europe, and as more and more people arrived in the United States as immigrants, they brought with them not only their joyfulness in the occasion of Christmas but also their traditional manners of celebration. One by one, beginning with Alabama in 1836, the states legalized the celebration of Christmas. Now it seems hard to believe that it has not always been so.

Many Christmas traditions have survived the centuries almost without change. One of the most enjoyable is the observance of Advent, a period of preparation for Christmas that, according to church calendar, begins the Sunday nearest to November 30. Another is the pleasure of making things by hand for the enjoyment of your family, your friends, and yourself. This book is a collection of traditional holiday decorations, foods, and other projects, one for each day of Advent, to keep or to give away.

DECEMBER 1 / ADVENT BANNER

The four Sundays before Christmas are observed in many Christian churches as the season of Advent, a time of quiet preparation for the joy and splendor of the Nativity, the coming of Christ into the world. ("Advent" is from Latin words meaning "to come.")

But outside the church and in the home, this period is less quiet. Popularly observed as the twenty-four days beginning December 1, Advent is a busy time of making gifts, sending cards, baking cookies, and so on. In many countries, it is customary to mark the passage of the days and weeks before Christmas. An Advent wreath with four candles is traditional in both homes and churches. Some people, particularly German children, count the days with Advent calendars, often elaborate scenes with tiny doors and windows that are opened, one on each day starting on December 1, to reveal a picture or a symbol.

There are many variations on the calendar idea, and the Advent banner is one of them. Each house along the winding road represents one of the twenty-four days of Advent, and the church at the top of the path is the climax of the season, Christmas Eve. Little figures—perhaps one for each member of your family—visit a new house each day until, at last, it's Christmas.

There are two ways of making this Advent banner. In Method I, the houses are cut from felt and are glued on the felt background. Extra details can be glued on too, or even drawn on with felt-tipped pens. This is a quick way to make the banner, and with several people working, it can be finished in no time.

In Method II, the houses are made of patches of cloth, each one hemmed and then stitched separately onto the cloth background. Extra details and decorations are embroidered on the patches and the background. This takes quite a lot of time, and it is a good project for a group of people to work on together.

METHOD I / GLUED-ON FELT

What You Will Need

Dark felt for background (preferably green or blue), 18 inches wide and about 5 feet long; 2 pieces of felt, 1 red and 1 white, each about 12 inches wide and 18 inches long, or several smaller pieces of various bright colors; white glue; several pieces of scrap paper for patterns; scissors, pencil, ruler; 3 yards decorative braid or thick yarn; 30 inches of string or yarn; 1 wooden dowel, 20 inches long.

Making the Banner

Make a pattern for the house and one for each of the two roof styles. For the house, cut a rectangular pattern 2 inches by 2½ inches. For the peaked roof, cut a 2½-inch square in half diagonally to form a triangle. For the flat roof, cut a rectangle 1 inch by 2½ inches and trim the ends to a slant.

Copy the pattern here for the church, following the measurements on the drawing.

Use the patterns to cut 23 houses, 12 peaked roofs, 11 flat roofs, and the church. Cut some of the houses and roofs of one color, some of others.

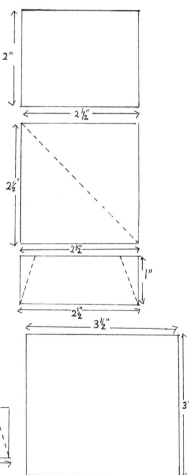

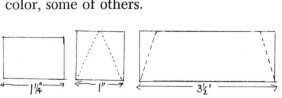

Use the braid or thick yarn to make a meandering zigzag path from the narrow bottom end of the background to the top, ending at the center of the top. Arrange the 23 houses along the path and the church at the top. Lay the peaked-roofed houses so that they are low and wide and the flat-roofed houses tall and narrow. One by one, spread glue evenly on the back of each house and press it in place. Then glue the path in place, a few inches at a time. Use two short lengths of yarn to put a cross on the church steeple.

If you have enough white felt left over, cut tall triangles, trim them into pine-tree shapes, and glue them in clumps among the houses.

Glue the top of the banner around the wooden dowel. Tie the string or yarn to the ends for hanging.

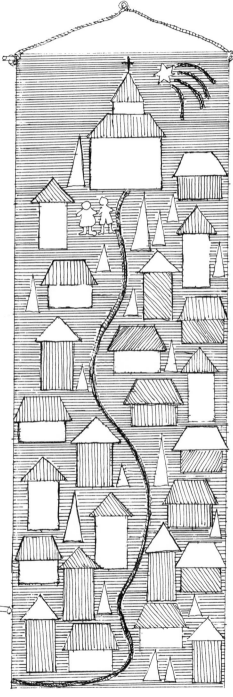

3

METHOD II / APPLIQUÉ

What You Will Need

Fairly heavy plain dark background fabric (preferably green or blue), 18 inches wide and about 5 feet long; scraps of bright-colored cloth, about 1 yard altogether; several pieces of scrap paper for patterns; needle, thread, scissors; pencil, ruler, straight pins, chalk; light-colored thin yarn and large needle to fit; 2 wooden dowels, each 18 inches long.

Making the Banner

Make a pattern for the house and each of the two roof styles. For the house, cut a rectangular pattern 2½ inches by 3 inches. For the peaked roof, cut a 3-inch square in half diagonally to form a triangle. For the flat roof, cut a rectangle 1½ inches by 3 inches and trim the ends to a slant. Copy the pattern on page 2 for the church, following the measurements on the drawing.

Use plain cloth for the houses and patterned cloth for the roofs, or the other way around. Or you can use all plain cloth in different colors. Use the patterns to cut 23 houses, 12 peaked roofs, 11 flat roofs, and the church.

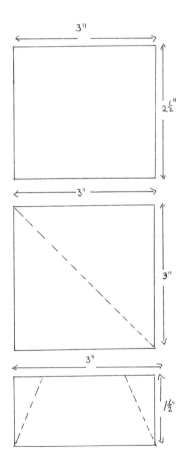

Turn under a ¼-inch hem on the cut edges of each piece and baste them with long running stitches, the simple in-and-out kind.

Cut the background cloth to size. Mark a ½-inch hem along each long side. Turn the hem to the back side. Turn under a little bit of the cut edge, and pin and baste it with large running stitches. Stitch it by machine or by hand with hemming stitches, angled stitches that go through both the edge of the hem and a few threads of the rest of the fabric. They should be so small that they barely show on the right side. Turn a 1-inch hem at the narrow top and bottom ends. Pin, baste, and stitch the hems.

With a piece of chalk, make a meandering zigzag path from the narrow bottom end of the background to the top, ending at the center of the top. Arrange the 23

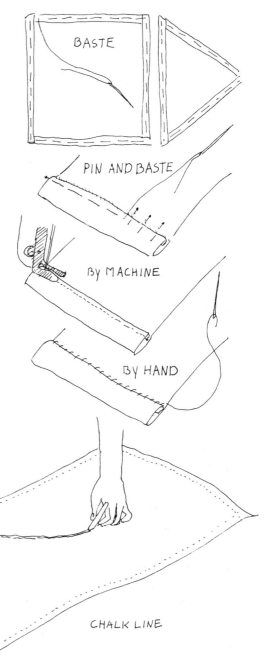

BASTE

PIN AND BASTE

BY MACHINE

BY HAND

CHALK LINE

houses along the path and the church at the top. Pin each house and roof in place. For the peaked-roofed houses, lay the rectangles so the houses are low and wide. For the flat-roofed houses, lay the rectangles so the houses are tall and narrow.

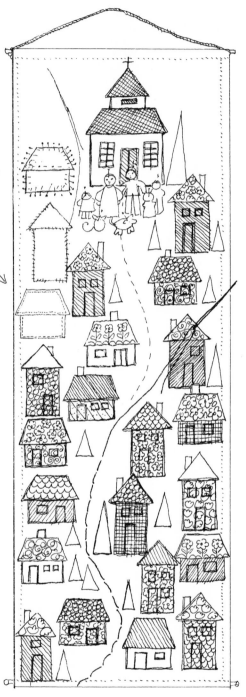

Sew each house and roof to the background by machine or by hand with hemming stitches. If you like, add doors, windows, and chimneys to the houses with yarn or embroidery thread, making one straight stitch for each line. Be sure to make a cross on top of the church steeple.

When all the houses and the church are in place, thread the large needle with yarn and stitch along the chalked path in running stitches. Make the stitches long on the right side of the cloth and short on the wrong side.

Slide the wooden dowels through the top and bottom hems. Tie a piece of yarn or string to the ends of the top dowel for hanging.

6

Making the Figures for Both Banners

Make little boy and girl figures with pipe cleaners, or cut them from scraps of felt or cloth or even from heavy paper. Pin the figures to the first house on the first day of December. Move the figures one house farther each day, until they reach the church on December 24.

An Advent banner makes an especially fine gift, because it can be saved and brought out again year after year. If you're making one to give to another family, be sure to include everybody in the family—maybe even the cat and dog!

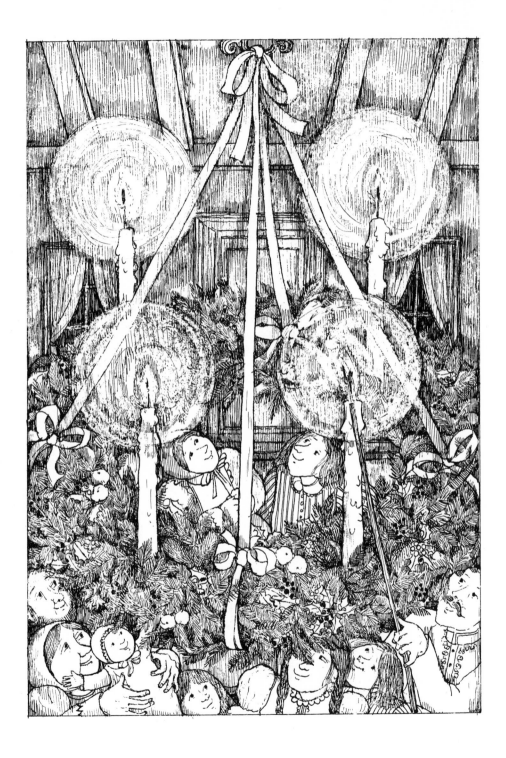

DECEMBER 2 / ADVENT WREATH

Candles are very much a part of the observance of Christmas, as they were in other religions. The Druids honored the sun god with lighted candles. The Romans used candles on trees during the Saturnalia. The ancient Hebrews celebrated Chanukah—the Feast of Lights—by lighting one candle each night for eight nights, and Jews today continue this custom. Jesus said, "I am the light of the world," and candles are used, not only at Christmas but on many other occasions, to represent Christ and his light.

Making a wreath of evergreen branches with four large candles, one to be lighted on each of the four Sundays of Advent, is a custom that is practiced in many homes and churches, particularly in Germany, England, and America. Some are big, elaborate affairs that hang from the ceiling; others are simple wreaths for the table.

You can make an Advent wreath with painted clay that can be used year after year. Use any kind of self-hardening clay, such as this familiar "play clay."

What You Will Need

1 cup cornstarch
2 cups baking soda
1¼ cups cold water
saucepan
spoon
waxed paper
damp cloth
4 thick candles
toothpick
green paint and brush
red and gold paint (optional)

Mixing the Clay

Mix the cornstarch and baking
soda in a saucepan. Add the water
slowly, mixing it well. Bring the
mixture to a boil and cook it
slowly for a few minutes, stirring
it as it cooks. It will be like mushy
mashed potatoes.

Scoop the mixture out with the
spoon onto a piece of waxed paper
and cover it with a damp cloth
to keep it from drying out as it

10

cools. When it is cool, knead the lump of clay by squeezing, turning, and folding it over and over as you would knead bread dough.

The clay is less likely to shrink and break apart if you make the wreath in sections that fit together so the whole thing can be taken apart for storage. Of course, this is a table wreath, not a hanging one.

First form four 2-inch balls of clay and mold one around the base of each candle, shaping the candleholder so that the candle will stand up steadily. Twist the candle gently to remove it without changing the shape of the molded candleholders.

1.

2.

4.

3.

11

Then make curved sections to fit between the candleholders so that the whole thing forms a wreath. Make them simple and flat or mold them like branches. Press the toothpick into the soft clay to make "evergreen needles" on the branches. Store the leftover clay in waxed paper.

When the parts are dry, paint them green. Add crisscrosses of red and gold, if you wish, to resemble ribbons. (You could also tie on real ribbons or yarn.) Put the candles in place.

12

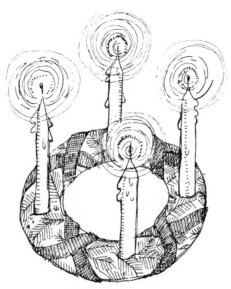

Light one candle on the first Sunday of Advent, two on the second, and so on, until all four candles are burning.

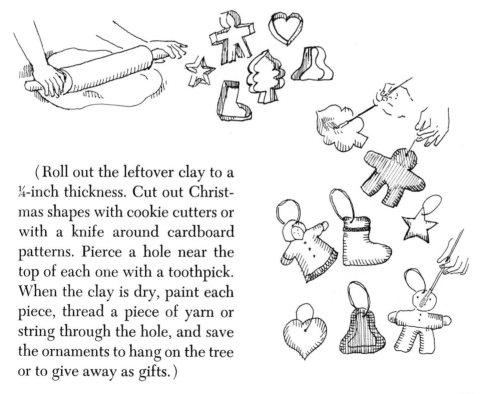

(Roll out the leftover clay to a ¼-inch thickness. Cut out Christmas shapes with cookie cutters or with a knife around cardboard patterns. Pierce a hole near the top of each one with a toothpick. When the clay is dry, paint each piece, thread a piece of yarn or string through the hole, and save the ornaments to hang on the tree or to give away as gifts.)

13

DECEMBER 3 / PAPER STARS

There are many stories about the origins of the Christmas tree. One legend tells of St. Boniface, an English missionary in Germany twelve centuries ago, who cut down an oak tree where a group of pagan worshipers were preparing to sacrifice a child. In place of the oak, a fir tree sprang up, and Boniface explained that it was the tree of Christ, a symbol of love.

The first written record of a Christmas tree appeared in a German manuscript at the beginning of the seventeenth century, describing a tree in Strasbourg which had been decorated with paper roses, apples, and sweets.

But some say the first Christmas tree was the inspiration of Martin Luther, the sixteenth-century leader of the Reformation in Germany. The legend goes that he was walking in the woods one snowy Christmas Eve, under a sky full of brightly shining stars. He cut down one of the small fir trees in the forest and took it home, where he set small candles on its branches, saying the flames reminded him of the stars in the heavens. The idea spread quickly, and other kinds of decorations were added to the candle glow. Two centuries after Martin Luther's tree was lighted, Hessian soldiers brought the custom of the Christmas tree from Germany to America during the Revolution.

Candles on a tree are very beautiful, but they are also very dangerous. However, you can make paper stars that are beautiful, reminders of the stars in the heavens, and not at all dangerous.

You can make the stars out of any kind of heavy paper in any color you like. A tree decorated with lots of white paper stars is very dramatic. Stars of different colors are a handsome addition to any tree. For shiny stars, glue together two squares of metallic gift-wrapping paper, shiny sides out. (Foil doesn't work well. It's too pliable to hold the shape.) Then proceed with the directions for folding.

What You Will Need

Heavy paper, pencil with eraser, scissors, ruler; heavy thread or string or yarn; large blunt-ended needle or other tool for punching a small hole (optional).

Making a Star

Draw a square on the paper, 4 inches wide and 4 inches long. Cut out the square. On the side you want to show, number each corner *lightly* with the pencil, like this:

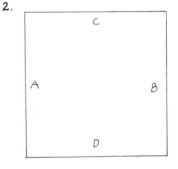

Then turn the square over and, on the reverse, letter each side like this:

Fold side A to side B. Press the fold firmly with your fingers. Open the square. Next fold side C to side D and press firmly.

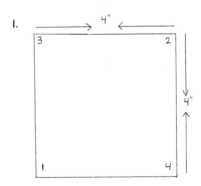

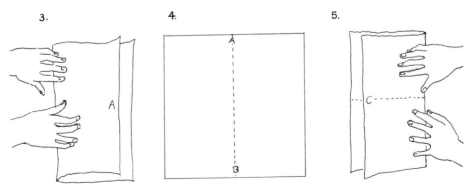

16

Open the square and turn it over. Now fold corner 1 to corner 2 and press the diagonal fold firmly.

Try making some stars that are bigger and some that are smaller. If you wish, you can decorate the stars with crayon or paints or glue-on glitter. After you make the first few, you won't need to number the corners or letter the sides to know how to make the folds. Make as many stars as you want for your tree to remind you of the stars that Martin Luther saw. (A boxful of stars could give a treeful of pleasure to someone on your gift list.)

Open the square. Fold corner 3 to corner 4 and press firmly. Open the square. Erase the penciled numbers. Pinch the corners gently to shape the 4-cornered star.

With the blunt-ended needle or other tool (a pencil point will do), punch a small hole at one of the corners. Cut a 6-inch piece of string, yarn, or heavy thread. Thread it through the hole and tie it in a loop for hanging.

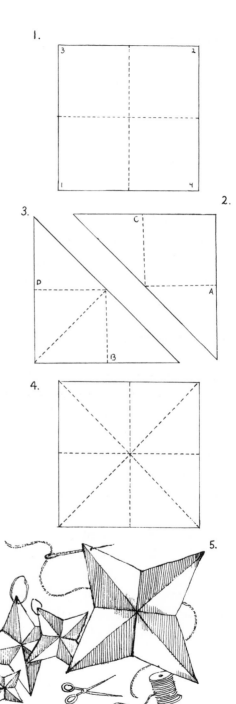

DECEMBER 4 / MACRAME KLOCKSTRÄNG

Bells have been used since ancient times to announce both happy and sad news. Many religions and many cultures have used bells for various reasons, and certainly bells have become especially associated with Christmas. In the sixth century, Christian churches began to ring bells to celebrate Christ's birthday; in the seventeenth century, New England town criers rang *their* bells to remind the Puritans that it was illegal to celebrate Christmas!

In Scandinavia, a favorite door decoration is the *klocksträng* or bellpull. Here is a version made by macrame, the ancient art of knotting ordinary string into unusual patterns. With the addition of a few bells, it becomes a gay *klocksträng* to hang near your front door, or to give as a gift.

What You Will Need

20 yards of red macrame yarn (sold in needlework and craft stores) or white cord or heavy string from the hardware store (knitting yarn is too stretchy); about 12 small bells; metal ring, belt buckle, or plain circle bracelet; 9 rubber bands, scissors, bright ribbon for bow (optional).

Making the Klocksträng

To make a rope about 16 inches long, cut 5 lengths of string, each 4 yards long. Fold one length of string exactly in half. Pull the loop formed at the center through the metal ring. Bring the two ends of the string up through the loop and pull the loop tight. Tie on the other lengths of string in the same way. Each piece of string is called an *end*. The 5 lengths of string make 10 ends.

Use a short piece of string to fasten the metal ring to a doorknob. This will anchor it firmly while you are tying the knots.

Each knot is made with four ends. The two ends used to tie the knot are the *working ends*. The ends around which the knots are tied are the *core ends*. The two ends in the center, #5 and #6, are core ends. Slide all the bells on these two ends together.

Then, starting at the bottom, wrap the two center core ends around your fingers to form a bobbin. When you have wound to within 18 inches of the metal ring, take your fingers out and fasten the bobbin with a rubber band. Wind all the other ends into separate bobbins. Unwind them as you need more string.

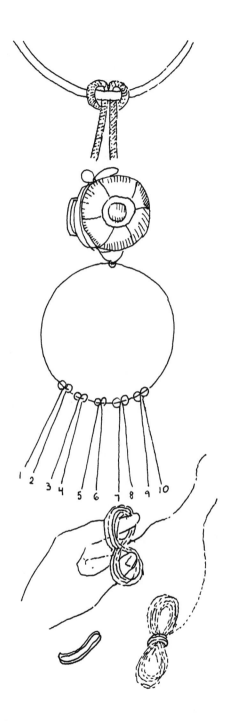

19

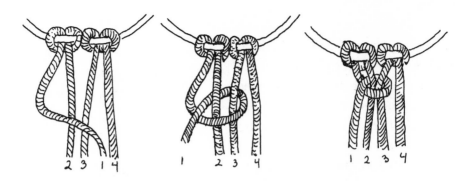

Although there are many macrame knots and combinations, you will be using only the left and right half hitch. For the first row of knots, start with working end #1 on the left and cross it loosely over the next two core ends, #2 and #3, forming a loop to the left. Bring #1 back under the core ends and up through the loop. Pull it tight. That makes a left half hitch.

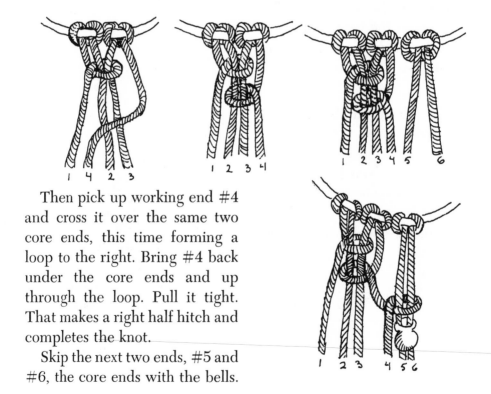

Then pick up working end #4 and cross it over the same two core ends, this time forming a loop to the right. Bring #4 back under the core ends and up through the loop. Pull it tight. That makes a right half hitch and completes the knot.

Skip the next two ends, #5 and #6, the core ends with the bells.

20

With the next four ends, make another knot with a left and right half hitch: Start with working end #7 and cross it over the two core ends, #8 and #9, forming a loop to the left. Bring #7 back under the core ends and up through the loop. That makes a left half hitch.

Then cross working end #10 over core ends #8 and #9, forming a loop to the right. Bring #10 back under the core ends and up through the loop. That makes a right half hitch.

In the next row, skip the first three ends. Then tie a left half hitch with working end #4, using #5 and #6 as core ends. Pull it tight and slide one of the bells along the core ends up close to the left half hitch. Tie a right half hitch with working end #7, to finish the knot and to hold the bell in place.

The third row is like the first.

The fourth row is like the second, also with a bell.

HOW PATTERN DEVELOPS ⟶

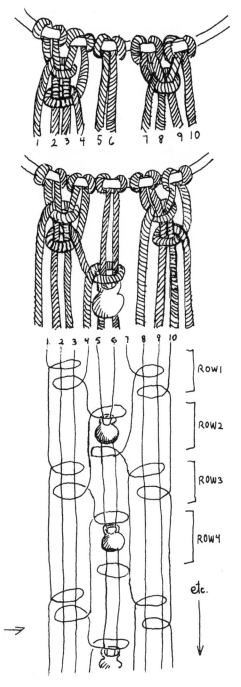

21

Keep on alternating rows, using a bell in every other row, until either the bells or the string is used up. (If you have only a few bells, use one every four rows, instead of every two.)

To finish off, tie each pair of ends by forming them into a loop and pulling the ends through the loop. Trim the ends to make an even fringe.

Tie a ribbon bow on the metal ring, if you like. Hang the *klocksträng* in a protected place near the front door.

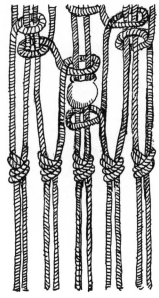

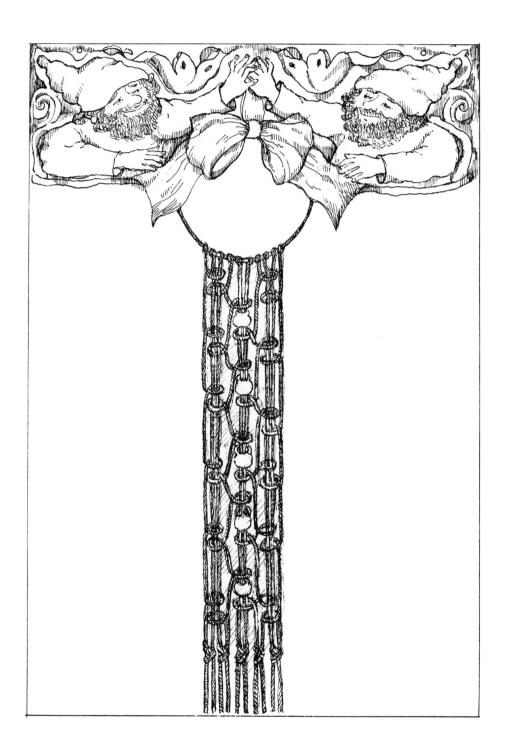

DECEMBER 5 / HOLLY-PRINTED WRAPPING PAPER

Holly had special significance among ancient people long before Christ was born. With its glossy green leaves and bright-red berries, it was considered sacred by the Druids thousands of years ago in the lands that are now France and England. The Romans gave each other holly wreaths during their celebration of the Saturnalia. The early Christians of Rome also used holly wreaths in order to look like everyone else and escape attention and punishment.

Eventually holly became a symbol of Christmas. With other evergreens, it was banned in Europe in the sixth century because of its pagan origins, but several hundred years later it again became a part of Christmas. There have been many superstitions about holly, which was said to produce everything from good luck and pleasant dreams to contented bees. But because it has come to stand for peace and happiness, it is enjoyed both as a beautiful plant and as an appropriate symbol of the season.

The holly leaf and berry are favorite designs for Christmas, and they lend themselves well to printing. You can print wrapping paper with a holly pattern, using only paints and an ordinary potato.

What You Will Need

Medium-sized raw potato, sharp kitchen knife, green and red tempera poster paints, pencil with eraser, small artist's brush, scrap paper, plain white shelf paper or white tissue paper.

Carving the Potato

Cut the potato in half with one even stroke of the knife to give it a smooth surface. With the edge of the knife, make a straight cut about ⅛ inch deep from one end of the potato surface to the other. Make a second cut, right beside it, slightly angled toward the first cut. Lift out the thin strip of potato.

Starting at one end of the cut line, cut out three curved sections along the edge of the potato, ending at the opposite end of the cut line. Then cut out three curved sections on the other side. This makes the general shape of a holly leaf. Blot away the potato juice. Cut a small piece of potato or use the pencil eraser for printing the holly berries.

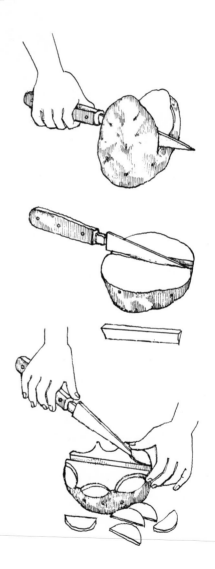

Printing with the Potato

With the brush, paint the cut surface of the potato evenly with green tempera paint. Then test it on a piece of scrap paper to find out how much paint you need and how hard you should press on the potato. Try printing three or four leaves, overlapping or just touching. When you have perfected your technique, use the potato to print bunches of holly leaves on the shelf paper or tissue paper. When the leaves have dried, use red paint and a small round potato stamp or the pencil eraser to make clusters of berries with each bunch of leaves.

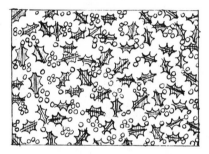

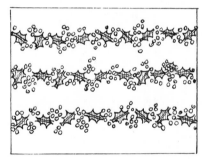

The design possibilities of potato printing are endless. Experiment with combining circles, squares, and odd shapes in different colors to come up with unusual patterns of your own.

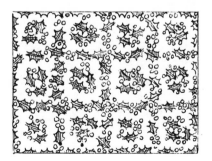

DECEMBER 6 / ST. NICHOLAS' DAY STOCKING

St. Nicholas is the ancestor of our own Santa Claus. Born of a noble family in Asia Minor in the fourth century, he became a priest. While still very young, he was made a bishop. Apparently he was a very good and kind bishop, for many legends sprang up about him, and his popularity spread.

The best-known story tells of three daughters of a poor man who were to be sold into slavery because their father did not have money for their dowries and so could not get husbands for them. Bishop Nicholas heard about their plight and, the story goes, he tossed three bags of gold through their window. One of the bags landed in a stocking that had been hung by the chimney to dry.

Within a century of the good bishop's death, he had been made a saint, and tales of his miracles spread through Europe. Hundreds of years later St. Nicholas was a favorite religious figure, and many countries and cities claimed him as their patron saint. He was pictured as a tall, slender, white-bearded man dressed in the costume of a bishop— a long white robe, a scarlet cape, and a red miter. The anniversary of his death, December 6, became an occasion for gift giving in many countries—especially the Netherlands. Sinterklaas, as he was called, was said to arrive on a white horse with presents for good children.

Eventually Sinterklaas emigrated to America, where his shape and costume, his personality, and even his name all changed dramatically. He became round and chubby with a jolly smile and twinkling eyes. He dressed in a fur-trimmed suit. He traded his horse for eight reindeer, the date of his appearance to December 24, and his old Dutch name to Santa Claus. But he is still known for his generosity, and a stocking hung by the chimney with care is almost certain to be found on Christmas morning stuffed with good things.

What You Will Need

For the pattern: newspaper, pencil, ruler, scissors, tape.
For the stocking: bright-red burlap or any other firm, tightly woven cotton fabric, about 14 inches wide and 18 inches long; thin white yarn or 6-strand embroidery floss (you may also use other color combinations); needle with an eye large enough for the yarn or 3 strands of floss at once to pass through; chalk, tape or straight pins, embroidery hoop, ordinary sewing needle, and thread to match the cloth; 4 inches of bright ribbon or yarn (optional).

Making the Stocking

For the pattern, cut a piece of newspaper 6 inches wide and about 23 inches long. Draw a line 10 inches from the bottom of the strip and fold the strip along the line. Then fold the smaller part of the strip on a diagonal so that the right edge of the smaller part is even with the fold, forming an "L." That makes the general shape of the stocking. Tape it so it doesn't unfold. Round off the "toe" and the "heel" with scissors.

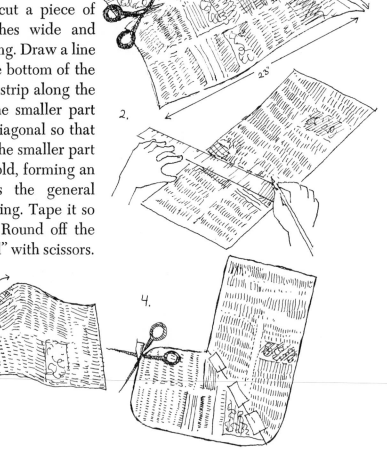

Lay the pattern on the cloth, placing it close to one edge to leave enough cloth for the other side of the stocking. Pin it or tape it down and draw around it with chalk. Remove the pattern. Do not cut it out yet.

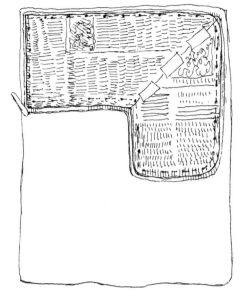

Then decide how you are going to decorate the stocking. Work out your design in pencil on the paper pattern and copy it onto the cloth with chalk.

Or use the design and the stitches shown here. For the band at the top of the stocking, draw line A 1½ inches from the top, line B 1 inch below line A, line C ½ inch below line B, and line D 1 inch below line C.

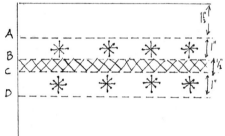

Put the embroidery hoop over the area you will be stitching. The hoop will hold the cloth taut. Cut a piece of yarn or three strands of embroidery thread about as long as your arm and thread the needle, leaving one end long and one short. Make a knot in the long end.

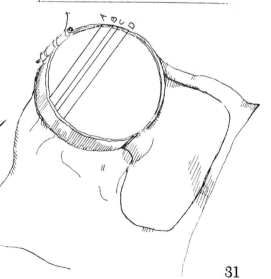

Embroidering the Stocking

Running stitch: Come up with the needle from the "wrong" (back) side of the cloth at the right end of line A. Stitch from right to left along the line with small, even stitches that are the same size on both sides of the cloth. Fasten off by winding the needle in and out of the stitches on the wrong side. Stitch lines B, C, and D in the same way.

Star stitch: Make three or four chalk dots, evenly spaced, between lines A and B. Keep the dots at least 1 inch away from the sides, which will be sewn together later. Come up with the needle about ¼ inch to the left of the first dot and go down about ¼ inch to the right of it. Come up again about ¼ inch below the dot and go down about ¼ inch above it. That makes a cross. Make another cross with its arms between the arms of the first cross. Then make a tiny third cross over the other two, to hold down the stitches in the center.

Make a second row of star stitches between line C and line D.

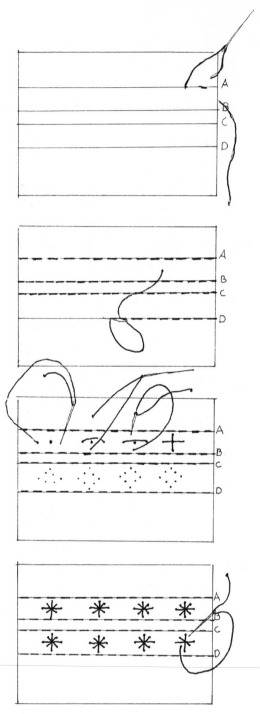

Cross stitch: Make a chalk mark on line C ½ inch from the left edge and call it #1. Make a chalk mark on line B 1 inch from the edge and call it #2. Make mark #3 on line C, directly beneath #2.

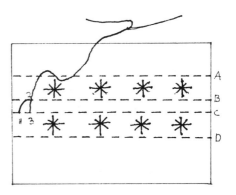

Come up with the needle at #1, go down at #2, and come up at #3, making one stitch. Make slanted stitches like the first one across the row, ending ½ inch from the right edge. That makes a row of half X's. Then work back across the row in the opposite direction, making the second half of the X's.

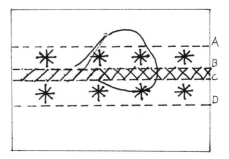

Back stitch: Print a name with chalk in large block letters on the foot of the stocking. Come up with the needle at the end of the last letter of the name. Make one running stitch, from right to left. Then go down again exactly where you went down for the first stitch and come up a little ahead of the second stitch. A stitch backward is part of each stitch forward. Skip from one letter to the next on the wrong side, so it doesn't show.

Sewing the Stocking

When you have finished the embroidery, cut out the stocking. (If the chalk outline has faded, pin the pattern on and cut around it.) Reverse the pattern and draw around a second piece. You can embroider this half to match the first or leave it plain. Then cut out the second piece.

With the right sides on the inside, put the two pieces together and pin them. Measure ½ inch all around the edges and mark with chalk. Using ordinary thread, sew all around the stocking with small running stitches. Leave the top open.

With your scissors, clip the seam carefully up near the stitches where the top of the foot makes a corner with the leg. Be careful to cut only up close to the stitches, not through them.

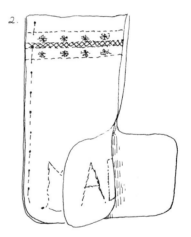

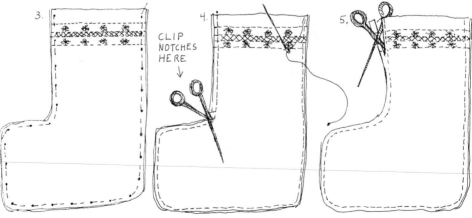

Turn down to the wrong side a ½-inch hem all around the top edge. Then turn under a little of the cut edge. Pin it and sew all around it with hemming stitches or tiny running stitches.

Cut a 4-inch piece of yarn or ribbon. Make a loop with it and sew it to the corner with several stitches on top of each other. Hang the stocking by the chimney for St. Nicholas's visit. Or make it for a younger child and give St. Nick a helping hand by stuffing the stocking yourself with inexpensive little toys, wrapped candies, a package of cookies (recipe on page 116)—and maybe a new toothbrush!

DECEMBER 7 / EARLY AMERICAN CRANBERRY LOAF

The recipes for most of the foods enjoyed at Christmas in this country came originally from somewhere else. One of the few strictly American contributions to Christmas is the cranberry. (Turkey was part of the holiday menu in parts of Europe in the sixteenth century. Spanish explorers had taken some of the birds back from Mexico.) Whether it's made into sauce or relish, baked in a bread, or strung on threads to decorate the tree, the cranberry has been an American favorite since the Indians introduced it to the white settlers.

Cranberry loaf is a simple, delicious, and inexpensive holiday fruit cake. It keeps well and makes a fine gift. Store it in the freezer until gift-giving time.

What You Will Need

Colander or strainer, 1 large mixing bowl, 2 small mixing bowls, food chopper or sharp knife, measuring cups and spoons, a 9×5×3-inch loaf pan, fork, 2 table knives, grater (optional), spoon, toothpick, potholders, wire rack, aluminum foil, and—

2 cups flour
1 cup sugar
1½ teaspoons baking powder
½ teaspoon baking soda
1 teaspoon salt
¼ cup soft shortening
1 egg

¾ cup orange juice *or* milk
½ cup nuts (optional)
1 orange, for grating rind
    (optional) or store-bought
    grated orange rind (optional)
2 cups cranberries (half of a
    1-pound box)

Making the Cranberry Loaf

Wash the cranberries in the colander or strainer. Pick out and discard any soft or brown ones. If you have a food chopper, use it to chop the berries. Otherwise, use the sharp knife to cut the cranberries in half a few at a time. (This is a tedious process, and it's nice to have someone help you.) Put them in a small mixing bowl. If you are using nuts, chop or break them up and put them in the same bowl.

Turn on the oven (or have someone help you do it) and let it heat to 350°.

With your fingers or a piece of paper towel, smear a dab of shortening all over the inside of the loaf pan, so that you can remove the finished loaf easily. Be sure not to miss any spots.

Put the flour, sugar, baking powder, baking soda, and salt in the large mixing bowl. Mix them lightly with the fork.

38

Add the rest of the shortening. With the 2 table knives, one in each hand, cut through the shortening to mix it with the flour mixture. Keep cutting it until it looks like coarse sand.

Break the egg into the second small mixing bowl and beat it well with the fork. Add either orange juice or milk and mix it well.

If you used orange juice and like more orange flavor, grate about 1 tablespoon of orange rind this way: Put a plate or a piece of waxed paper under the grater. Rub the orange against the fine teeth of the grater just enough to remove the orange outside layer. Don't grate the white part. Keep turning the orange until you have grated enough peel. Or you can use grated orange rind from the spice rack of the grocery store. Add it to the orange juice and egg.

Add the egg mixture to the flour mixture. Mix it in with the fork just enough to dampen the flour. Don't try to mix it smooth.

Add the cranberries and nuts and stir them carefully into the batter.

Use the spoon to spread the batter into the loaf pan. Smooth the top of the loaf and make the corners a little higher than the center, because it will rise most in the center.

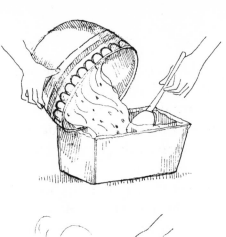

Bake the loaf for 1 hour. When the top is golden brown, stick the toothpick into it. If it comes out clean, the loaf is finished. Use the potholders to take it out of the oven. When it is cool enough to handle, remove it from the pan and set it on a wire rack until it is completely cool. Wrap it tightly in aluminum foil. Put it in the freezer if you plan to keep it for more than a few days before it is eaten or given away.

Wait at least one day before slicing it. Serve it plain, with butter, or with cream cheese. It's good toasted, too.

Making Cranberry Sauce

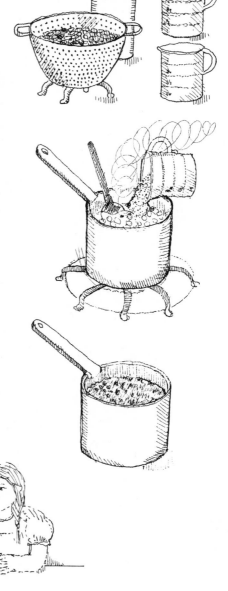

If you want to make cranberry sauce with the two remaining cups of berries in the box, you'll need only a saucepan, spoon, bowl or jar, 1 cup of sugar, and ¾ cup water.

Mix the two cups of washed cranberries (be sure to throw out any soft or brown ones) with the sugar and water in a saucepan. Bring the mixture to a boil and cook it for about five minutes, until all the cranberries have popped open. Turn off the burner.

Let the sauce cool in the pan for a half hour or so. Then pour it into the bowl or jar. Cover it with a lid and store it in the refrigerator.

DECEMBER 8 / STENCILED GREETING CARDS

In the early part of the nineteenth century, English schoolchildren were often required to produce "Christmas pieces" for their parents. These formal letters had seasonal decorations in the borders, and the purpose was to show the young pupils' progress in handwriting as well as to wish their families a merry Christmas.

Then, in the 1840s, several people at about the same time had the idea of having cards printed up with Christmas scenes and greetings, and they mailed the cards to their friends. Soon several printing companies had taken up the idea and were making such cards, but they were expensive and only the rich could afford them. As printing methods were improved and postage rates were reduced, the custom became more popular.

About a hundred years ago, Louis Prang, a German immigrant, began printing Christmas cards in his shop in Massachusetts. Now Christmas cards are a huge industry in this country, but handmade cards are still the most treasured of all. You can make a stencil and print all the cards you need.

What You Will Need

White or colored construction paper or other stiff paper; scrap paper, pencil, ruler, scissors, old newspapers, paper clips, sponge, saucer; tempera poster paints in one or more colors that show up well on the paper; felt-tipped pen; seals, bright tape, or envelopes; postage stamps.

Making the Cards

If you are using envelopes, cut a piece of scrap paper that will fit in the envelope when it is folded once. (For instance, for a 3½-by-6½-inch envelope, cut a piece 6½ by 6 inches and fold it to 3¼ by 6 inches.) Use the unfolded paper as a model for cutting as many cards as you need.

If you don't have envelopes, you can make double-folded cards that form their own envelopes. Fold sheets of 8½-by-11-inch typing paper in half crosswise, putting the fold at the top. Or cut pieces of construction paper about 9 by 6 inches. Measure 2½ inches from each end and fold the ends toward the center. Use the inside middle panel for printing. Then, when you're ready to mail the card, use seals, stickers, or tape to fasten the two side panels.

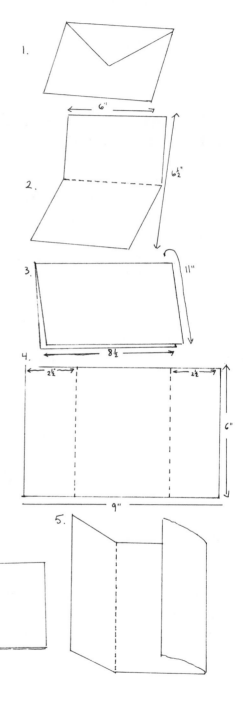

In stenciling, the painting is done in one or more colors through a cutout design. To make the stencil, cut a piece of stiff paper the size of the area to be printed. Decide whether you want to use the area horizontally with the fold at the top, or vertically with the fold at the left. Then work out a design to fit the area.

For a simple tree design, fold the stencil paper in half and tear or cut one half of the tree along the fold. Start narrow at the top and gradually broaden it toward the bottom.

Or fold the paper in quarters and cut out a star design.

You can also draw a design on the paper and cut it out with small sharp scissors. Keep the shapes as simple as possible.

For more complicated patterns, make an additional stencil for each part of the design; after the first printing has dried, overprint it with a second stencil, using another color. For example, print a tree in green on white paper. Using one of the prints as a stencil, punch holes in the tree for Christmas ornaments and overprint the ornaments on the trees with red.

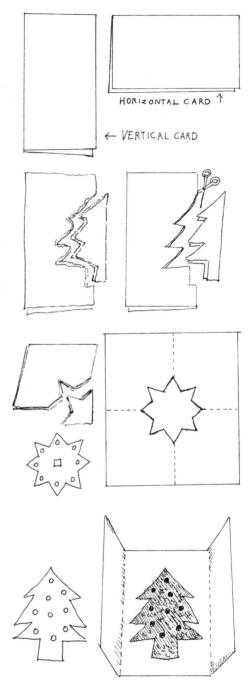

HORIZONTAL CARD ↑

← VERTICAL CARD

Do the stenciling with a sponge, which will give a pebbly, textured effect. Put down several layers of old newspapers to protect your work surface from paint drips. Pour a little paint in a saucer. Cut a piece of sponge about 1 inch wide and 3 inches long. Wet the sponge with water and squeeze it out well.

Lay the stencil over the part of the card that is to be printed and fasten it at top and bottom with paper clips. Dip the end of the sponge in the paint and dab it lightly over the cutout part of the stencil. Be sure to cover the entire area (you're bound to get some paint on the stencil too, which is all right). Lift off the stencil carefully and set the card aside to dry. (It is a good idea to try a few practice printings before you begin on the cards, to find out how much paint you need to give the effect you want.)

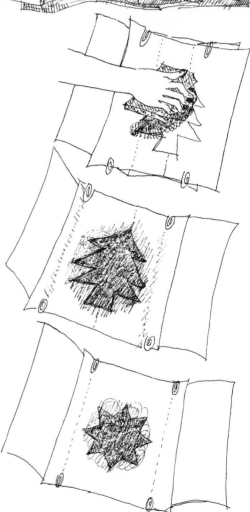

46

When the paint is completely dry, add an overprinting, if you wish.

Write a greeting inside the single-fold cards or on the inside panels of the double-fold cards.

Refold the cards and put them in the envelopes, or seal the two flaps of the self-mailing kind with bright seals or tape. Put the name, address, and postage on the opposite side.

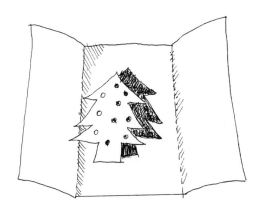

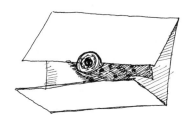

DECEMBER 9 / GOD'S EYES

The Huichol Indians of Mexico and the Aymará of Bolivia weave bright-colored yarn on a simple frame of crossed sticks to make a design called the *Ojo de Dios,* or Eye of God. At one time, God's Eyes were made to be placed on an altar so that the gods could watch over the praying people. Although they were not originally made for Christmas, God's Eyes are unusual and attractive holiday decorations.

What You Will Need

2 Popsicle sticks or other short, smooth sticks; knitting yarn in 2 or 3 bright Christmas colors; scissors, pencil; small bells (optional).

Making the God's Eye

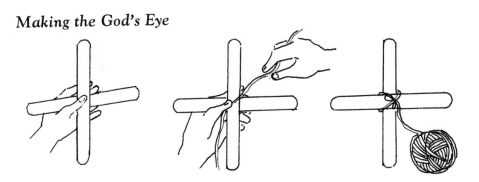

Cross the sticks at the centers. Tie them together with the end of a piece of yarn, making an X, but don't cut the yarn off its ball or skein. Tie the yarn in back of the crossed sticks. With the pencil, number the sticks about halfway from the center, like this:

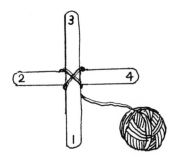

Bring the yarn to the front between any two sticks—say 3 and 4. Pull the yarn over stick 3 and the next one too (stick 2) and bring it to the back between 2 and 1. Wrap it behind 2 and bring it to the front again between 2 and 3. Pull it over 2 and the next one too (stick 1) and wrap it behind stick 1. Pull it over 1 and the next one too (stick 4) and wrap it behind stick 4. Pull it over 4 and the next one too (stick 3) and wrap it behind stick 3. This is one round. Always lay the yarn next to, not on top of, the yarn already in place.

Keep on wrapping the yarn behind each stick, over that stick and the next, and around behind that one, then over that stick and the next, and behind that one.

As you continue making the rounds, always be sure that the yarn lies next to, but never on top of, the yarn in the previous round. After the first few rounds you will see the woven pattern beginning to form. When you have an "eye" in one color of yarn, you can cut the yarn, tie on another color, and continue weaving. Make sure the knot stays in the back.

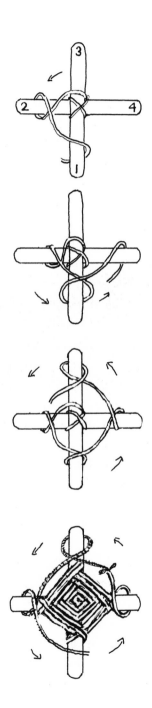

49

Keep on weaving the God's Eye until you are ½ inch from the ends of the sticks. Cut the yarn, leaving a 7-inch tail. Tie the tail in a knot in back of the last stick that you wrapped. Use the long remaining tail to make a loop for hanging.

A God's Eye of this size is an unusual tree ornament. You can also make much smaller ones—with toothpicks and string, for instance—but the tiny ones are harder to handle. And you can make a larger, more complicated God's Eye by crossing two large sticks—12 or more inches long—and then crossing a short stick at the end of each long one. Weave out only about two inches from the center of 12-inch sticks, farther on longer ones. Tie bells on the ends, if you have them, just for fun.

Weave the center part first. Then weave each of the four smaller Eyes. This large *Ojo de Dios* makes a handsome decoration to hang in a window—your own or the window of the friend to whom you give it as a gift.

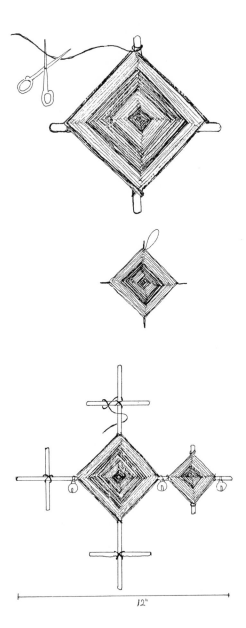

DECEMBER 10 / GINGERBREAD COTTAGE

The gingerbread house, made of spicy cookie dough and trimmed with icing, is a Christmas tradition in many European homes. The house can be very elaborate, and sometimes people who have spent a lot of time making very fancy ones decide they are just too pretty to eat and keep them year after year. But most people like to have the fun both of making the house and of eating it after Christmas.

Here is a small gingerbread cottage made in the form of an "A-frame," a popular style among people who build vacation houses because it is easy to put together. That makes it a good style for building a gingerbread cottage, too.

What You Will Need

For the pattern: heavy paper, ruler, pencil, scissors.
For the dough: 2 medium-sized mixing bowls, measuring cups and spoons, spoon and fork for mixing, pancake turner, rolling pin, small sharp knife, cookie sheet, potholders, wire rack, and—

½ cup molasses	½ teaspoon baking soda
4 tablespoons sugar	½ teaspoon salt
2 tablespoons vegetable oil	½ teaspoon cinnamon
2 tablespoons milk or water	½ teaspoon ginger
2 cups flour, plus a few table- spoons more	

For the icing: small mixing bowl, spoon, table knife, and—

1 cup powdered sugar	water

For the decorations: flat plate or tray; aluminum foil or colored paper; red cinnamon candies, silver dragees, gumdrops, or other candy decorations.

Making the Pattern

Draw a rectangle on the heavy paper 2 inches by 3½ inches for the base. Draw a rectangle 3 inches by 5 inches for the roof. Draw a triangle that is 4 inches along the base and 4½ inches high for the front and back of the cottage. (To draw the triangle, first draw the base line. Measure 2 inches in from the end of the line and make a mark. Measure 4½ inches straight up from the mark and make a second mark. Draw lines from the second mark to each end of the base line.)

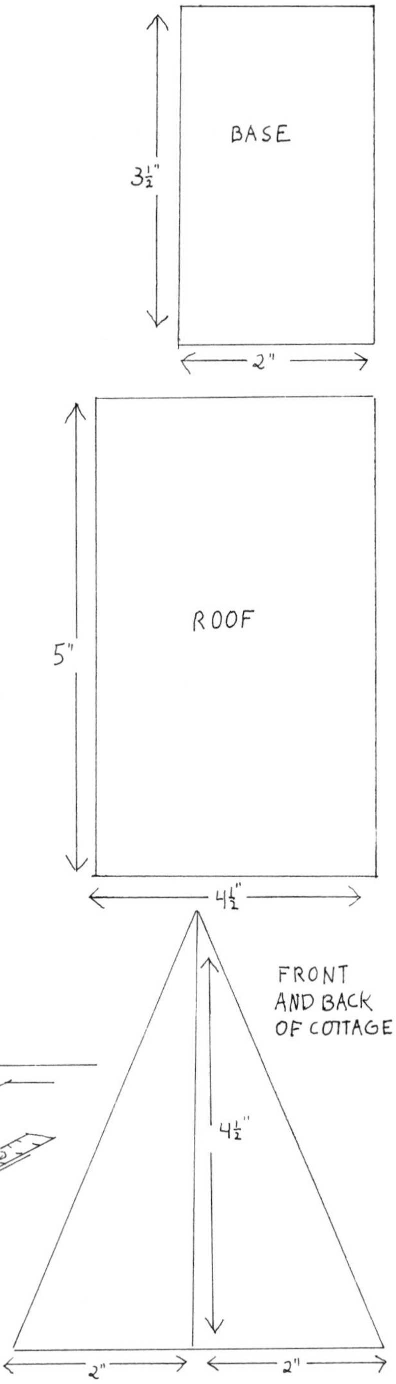

BASE

3½"

2"

ROOF

5"

4½"

FRONT AND BACK OF COTTAGE

4½"

2"   2"

Making the Dough

In one bowl, put the molasses, sugar, vegetable oil, and milk or water. Mix them well with a spoon.

In the other bowl, put the dry ingredients—2 cups of the flour, the baking soda, salt, cinnamon, and ginger. Mix them lightly with the fork.

Add the dry ingredients gently to the molasses mixture, about ⅓ at a time, and stir well with the spoon after each addition. Use your hands to work in a little more flour if you need it to make a dough that is stiff but not crumbly. Or add a little more milk or water if the dough crumbles. Form the dough into a ball.

Cutting Out the Pieces

Sprinkle most of the remaining flour on the table or counter where you will be rolling out the dough. Dust a little more flour on the rolling pin. Flatten the ball of dough on the floured table with your hand. Then roll it out flat with the rolling pin. The rolled-out dough should be between ⅛ and ¼ inch thick.

Turn on the oven (or have someone help you do it) and let it heat to 350°.

Use the paper patterns to cut out the parts of the cottage. Lay the patterns on the rolled-out dough and cut around them carefully with the sharp knife. Cut one base rectangle, two roof rectangles, and two triangles for the front and back. Use the pancake turner to lift the cut-out dough pieces carefully and place them on the cookie sheet. If the pieces get out of shape in the process, try to coax them gently back into shape.

After the parts are arranged on the cookie sheet, use the knife to cut out a small door at the bottom of one triangle and a small window in the center of the other. Bake the pieces for 10 minutes.

While the pieces are baking, roll out the scraps and cut more shapes—regular cookie shapes or trees and animals to stand around the cottage.

When the pieces are finished baking, use the potholders to take the cookie sheet out of the oven. Let the pieces cool a few minutes on the cookie sheet so they can begin to harden. Use the pancake turner to transfer them to the wire rack to finish cooling. Then bake the other shapes the same way.

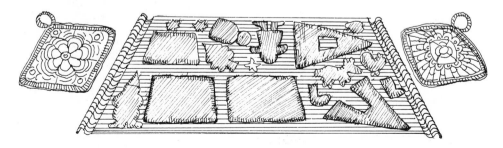

Making the Icing

While the pieces cool, mix the icing that you will use to cement the parts of the house together. Put the powdered sugar in the small bowl and add two teaspoonfuls of water. Mix well. Add more water, a few drops at a time, until you have made a thick paste, like cement.

Decorating the Pieces

Before you begin to put the pieces together, cut two squares of aluminum foil or colored paper slightly larger than the door and window and stick them to the openings on the "wrong" (back) side of the cookies with icing. Then turn the cookie parts over and stick on the candy decorations around the window and door.

Building and Decorating the Cottage

With the table knife, spread icing on the two long edges of the base rectangle. Put the base on the flat plate or tray. Stick a triangle on

each long side of the base, with the tall point up. Hold the triangles in place until the icing hardens and the triangles will stand up by themselves. This takes a couple of minutes. It pays to be patient.

Then spread icing thickly in wide stripes along each long side of the roof rectangles. Prop the roof rectangles in place against the two sides of the triangles. Hold them while the icing hardens.

After the cottage has been built and the "cement" has hardened, spread the rest of the icing over the roof of the house to resemble snow. You can push more candy decorations into the "snow." Make a little garden around the house with candy and gingerbread trees. Sprinkle the entire scene with more powdered-sugar snow.

Try not to eat the gingerbread cottage until everyone else has had a chance to admire it. But the gingerbread dries out and hardens in a few days, so unless you plan to save it, don't let too much time go by before you eat it.

DECEMBER 11 / GINGERBREAD SCULPTURE

Gingerbread that isn't made into houses often winds up in the form of boys, girls, animals, and other figures. You don't need special cookie cutters to make these cookies. The dough is like clay, and you can mold it to make whatever shapes you want.

What You Will Need

One recipe for Gingerbread Cottage dough (page 53); 2 cookie sheets; toothpick, potholders, pancake turner, wire rack.

Modeling the Figures

The dough should be rather soft, like clay. If it seems too dry and crumbly, add a few drops of water.

Then start modeling figures right on the cookie sheets. To make a gingerbread boy, begin with two round pieces of dough—medium-sized for the head, large for the body. Flatten the balls with the palms of your hands to a thickness of about ¼ inch. Make sure the two parts are securely joined at the neck.

When you are adding arms and legs, start with two pieces of dough that are about the same size, so they are more likely to match. Press them firmly against the body piece, so they won't break off so easily.

Add little bits and crumbs of dough for hair. Use the toothpick to draw on eyes and a smile. Draw them in deeply. As the cookie bakes, it rises a little and fills in little holes and scratches. Be sure all the parts of the cookie are about ¼ inch thick.

When you make a gingerbread girl, shape the body so that it has a skirt. Give her lots of hair. Make tiny buttons down the front.

Fish and birds are basically simple shapes. You can roll tiny pieces of dough between your fingers to make scales on the fish and feathers on the bird.

61

If you're planning to hang these cookies on the tree, use the toothpick to poke a hole near the top for a hanging string (put the string through *after* the cookies have been baked and cooled).

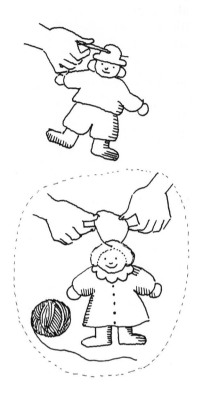

Turn on the oven (or have someone help you do it) and let it heat to 350°. Bake the gingerbread sculptures for about 10 minutes, then use the potholders to take the cookie sheets out of the oven. Let them cool for a few minutes on the cookie sheets so that they have a chance to harden. Then lift them carefully with the pancake turner and put them on the wire rack to finish cooling. Store them in a tightly covered container to keep them from drying out and becoming too hard to bite.

DECEMBER 12 / CHRISTMAS EGGS

The egg, a symbol of new life, is usually associated with Easter and the Resurrection of Christ, but in many places the egg also appears at Christmastime for the same reason. Decorated eggs hang on Christmas trees in many European countries.

What You Will Need

White eggs; washcloth, large needle, spoon, cup; yarn or ribbon; scissors; white glue; watercolor paints or food coloring, and an artist's paintbrush or felt-tipped pen.

How to Empty the Eggs

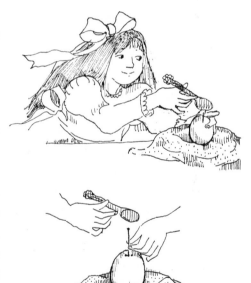

Eggs are fragile, but with a little patience you can empty them without breaking the shells. Dampen the washcloth and make a little "nest" to hold the egg upright. (And, in case the worst *does* happen, it makes the cleaning up easier.)

Hold the needle straight up and down over one end of the egg, point down, and tap it with the spoon to make a tiny hole in the egg. Make another hole next to the first one. Then make a third hole between those two, so that the three combine to make one small opening.

Turn the egg over and make the same kind of opening in the other end. Push the needle as far into the egg as you can without losing it. This breaks the yolk and makes it easier to blow it out.

Hold the egg over the cup and blow *hard* into one of the holes. Try not to squeeze the egg while you're blowing. If you have too much trouble blowing out the insides of the egg, use the needle to enlarge one of the holes a little and try again.

When the egg is empty, rinse it well under cool running water and dry it gently.

Decorating the Eggs

A plain white egg, tied with a piece of white or bright-colored knitting yarn or ribbon and hung on the tree, is a decoration of beautiful simplicity. Use tiny dabs of glue to anchor the yarn. You can also paint the eggs with watercolors in bright colors and designs.

Another possibility is to make a "scenic egg." To do this, start a hole in the side of the empty egg with the needle. Then, with your fingers, gently enlarge the hole, making it as even as possible, until it is a little over 1 inch high and almost that wide. Use a brush to paint the inside of the eggshell with watercolors, preferably in a light color.

Then cut a tiny figure—an angel or a star, for example—out of paper, or cut a tiny picture from a card or magazine. Put a dab of glue on the back of the cutout. Dampen your finger just enough so that the cutout will cling to it, and guide it gently into place inside the egg. Glue a loop of yarn or ribbon to one end of the egg for hanging.

To give an egg to a friend as a present, make a safe nest for it in a box lined with crushed tissue paper or cotton.

67

DECEMBER 13 / ST. LUCIA BUNS

In Sweden, St. Lucia's Day—December 13—is celebrated as a "Little Yule," the beginning of the holiday season and almost as important as Christmas itself. Lucia was born not in Sweden but in Sicily, where, according to legend, as a young girl she gave all her dowry money to the poor. This was such an unusual thing to do that she was accused of being a witch and was burned at the stake in the year A.D. 304. But even after her death, it was said, she went on helping those in need.

In some way the story of the saint from warm Sicily reached cold Sweden. Some say that she once fed the hungry in a part of Sweden that was suffering from a famine. Now her feast day is observed by young girls who dress as "Lucia brides" in long white gowns with crowns of candles on their heads and serve sweet buns called "Lucia cats" to their parents and friends.

Saffron gives the "cats" their yellow color and special flavor, but it is a very expensive spice and can be left out. You can use a few drops of yellow food coloring instead, or leave the buns plain. They will taste just as good. In any case, allow about half a day for making Lucia cats. Most of that is rising time for the dough, and you're free to do other things while you wait. This recipe makes 20 to 24 buns.

What You Will Need

For the buns: large mixing bowl, small saucepan, coffee cup (if you use saffron), measuring cups and spoons, large mixing spoon, rolling pin, small sharp knife, 2 cookie sheets, potholders, pancake turner, wire rack, freezer wrap or aluminum foil, and—

½ teaspoon powdered saffron (optional) or yellow food coloring (optional)
hot water
1 egg
1 cup milk

3½ cups flour
1 package dry yeast
¼ cup sugar
1 teaspoon salt
4 tablespoons soft shortening
raisins

For the icing: small mixing bowl, spoon, and—

1 cup powdered sugar   milk

Making the Buns

This dough is made with yeast, which is a living plant and needs warmth, but not too much warmth. You should be careful that the liquid you use is neither too hot nor too cold.

If you are using saffron in the buns, put it in a cup and add a teaspoonful of hot water to dissolve it.

Put the egg (still in the shell) in a bowl of lukewarm water to warm it slightly.

Heat the milk slowly in the saucepan until it feels warm but not hot.

Set the warmed egg aside, and rinse the mixing bowl with very warm water. Mix one cup of the flour with the yeast, sugar, and salt in the warmed bowl.

Add the warm milk, the shortening, and the dissolved saffron or a few drops of yellow food coloring. Stir the mixture until it is smooth.

Add the egg and a second cup of flour and mix well.

Add the rest of the flour and mix it with your hands until all the flour is worked in and you can form a ball with the dough. You can add a little more flour if it's still sticky.

Sprinkle some flour on your hands and on the table or counter where you are working. Put the ball of dough on the table and knead it this way: Flatten the ball, fold it in half, and press down on it hard with the heels of your hands to flatten it again.

Turn the circle of dough partway around and fold it and flatten it again. Keep turning, folding, and flattening the dough until it seems elastic, adding a little flour if the dough is sticky. Thorough kneading makes bread with a fine, even texture.

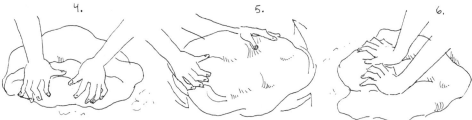

Wash the mixing bowl, dry it, and grease it lightly with shortening. Form the dough into a ball, grease the top of it, and put it in

the bowl. Note the size of the ball —when it has finished rising, it will be about double that size.

Cover the bowl lightly with a damp cloth and put it in a warm place (near a radiator or in a sink of warm water, for instance, but not on a hot burner).

The warmth helps the yeast to form bubbles of carbon dioxide gas, which causes the bread to rise. Depending on the temperature of the room, it will take about an hour and a half for the dough to double in size. (Check on it at the end of an hour.) When the dough has doubled, punch it down a few times with your fist. Cover it again and let it rise for another half hour until it has almost doubled again. Punch down the dough a second time, put the ball of dough on the table, and let it "rest" for five minutes.

Then, with a rolling pin, roll out the dough to a thickness of ¼ inch. Cut the dough in strips ½ inch wide. Cut each strip into pieces 4 inches long. Knead the leftover bits together, roll them out, and cut them into more 4-inch strips.

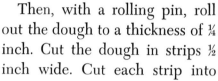

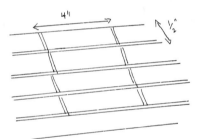

Lightly grease the cookie sheet. On the sheet make an X with two strips of dough. Curl both ends of each strip and put a raisin in each end. Do the same for each bun.

Turn on the oven (or have someone help you do it) and let it heat to 400°, while the buns rise for the third time on the cookie sheet on the table. This rising will take about 20 minutes.

Bake the buns for 10 to 12 minutes, until they are golden brown.

Use the potholders to take the cookie sheets out of the oven. Use the pancake turner to transfer the buns to the wire rack to cool for 15 minutes.

While they are still warm, you can spread them with icing. Put the powdered sugar in the small bowl and add two teaspoonfuls of milk. Stir it in. Add more milk, a few drops at a time, until you have a thick paste. Spread some on each Lucia "cat." Snugly wrapped in foil or freezer wrap, these "cats" can be frozen, then eaten or given away on another day. Warm them in the oven before you eat them.

DECEMBER 14 / POMANDER BALL

The first Christmas gifts were given to the Christ Child by the "Three Kings," actually priests and astrologers, who followed the Star and reached Bethlehem twelve days after Jesus was born. The day of their arrival is called Epiphany, meaning "manifestation" or "being made known." The Three Kings brought with them precious gifts of gold, frankincense, and myrrh. The last two are kinds of incense treasured for their aroma.

The custom of giving gifts at the season we celebrate as Christmas began in pre-Christian Roman times, during the Saturnalia. Because gift giving at this time of year was considered a pagan habit, the early Christians did not practice it. However, it's such a nice custom that by the twelfth century many people were giving each other gifts at Christmas—or at least at some time during the season. In some places Epiphany—January 6—is gift-giving day. Some people exchange on January 1. St. Nicholas' Day, December 6, is the occasion for others.

There are different "gift bringers," too. In America, of course, it's Santa Claus, while his ancestor, St. Nicholas, visits many European homes. Father Christmas makes the rounds in England. In Germany it's the *Christkind* or Christ Child, dressed in a long white robe. In Sweden and Denmark the job is taken over by elves, the *tomten* and the *nisse*. Befana, an old woman, visits Italian children and leaves gifts with them. Père Noël—Father Christmas—comes to France, and in many places it's the Three Kings themselves who bring the gifts.

Even with all these gift bringers roaming the world, the best presents still seem to be exchanged among relatives and friends. A pomander ball is an especially appropriate gift. "Pomander" originally meant "amber apple." It was a hollow ball filled with spices and was worn around the neck as a protection from illness. Present-day pomander balls are made of real apples and we know they serve no medicinal purpose. But their spicy aroma is pleasant in a closet or drawer, and it's a reminder of the aromatic gifts brought to the first Christmas child.

What You Will Need

Apple, 1 box of whole cloves, cinnamon, ginger, small paper bag, yarn or ribbon, newspapers.

Making a Pomander Ball

Spread out the newspapers and put the apple on them. Push the stems of the cloves all the way into the apple, fitting them as close together as you can, until the whole apple is completely covered. Put a little cinnamon and ginger into the paper bag with the apple, close the top of the bag, and shake it until the apple is coated with the spices. Tie a piece of yarn or ribbon around the apple and make a loop at the top for hanging.

Pomander balls last indefinitely without rotting or molding, because the cloves help draw all the moisture out of the apple. But they do lose their spicy smell after a while.

DECEMBER 15 / CHRISTMAS TERRARIUM

Living plants have long been a part of Christmas. People like to give and receive plants as gifts. The bright-red-"flowered" poinsettia, brought to the United States from Mexico a hundred years ago, is an American favorite. Some people start narcissus and hyacinth bulbs indoors so that they will bloom in December. The Christmas cactus, which can be brought to bloom once a year at Christmas, is popular. Long ago laurel (or bay, as it's sometimes called) and rosemary, both now known mostly in cooking, were Christmas plants.

Mistletoe, holly, and ivy—as well as evergreens—have been symbols of life since long before the birth of Christ. Although ivy is not used at Christmas in the United States, it is popular in England. In old English custom, holly was thought to be masculine and ivy feminine. A traditional carol, "The Holly and the Ivy," celebrates their affinity.

A terrarium—a miniature garden in a glass container—is a fascinating way to enjoy living plants at Christmas, using holly and ivy or whatever plants you choose. (Because the holly sprigs do not have roots, they will last only a few weeks in the terrarium. Then they can be removed and other plants put in their place.) A terrarium will continue to give pleasure long after the tinsel and colored lights have been put away for another year.

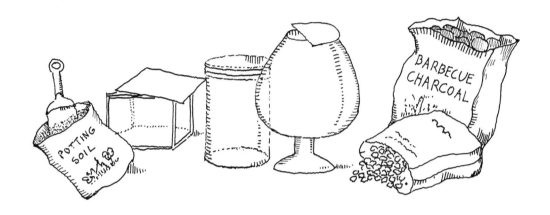

What You Will Need

Almost any kind of clear glass container can be used—a goldfish bowl, an aquarium, or a large jar such as a peanut-butter jar with a mouth wide enough to put your hand through. The container should have a lid or some kind of covering for the opening to keep the moisture inside. A glass or hardware store can cut a piece of glass to fit an aquarium (it should be a little shorter than the length of the aquarium and a little wider than the aquarium). The jar lid or a piece of cardboard can be painted with acrylic enamel paint or covered with foil.

You'll need enough gravel to cover the bottom of the container to a depth of about 1 inch. Any kind or size will do. Aquarium gravel is good, if you have it, but you can collect little pebbles by the roadside. Wash them thoroughly to remove chemicals and pollutants.

Charcoal is not absolutely necessary, but it helps to keep the water and soil sweet in a terrarium and prevents the growth and decay of green algae. If you have a bag of charcoal for barbecuing, you can use some of the broken bits and particles. It is also available in packages of granules at garden-supply stores.

Use ordinary soil from your garden, if it has not been frozen too hard to dig up. Or buy potting soil from a garden-supply store.

The plants you use depend on what you can find and what you like. They should be small plants with small leaves. If the ground is not yet completely frozen in your area, you can dig up small wild plants (be sure to dig up the roots, too). Even if there's snow on the ground, you may be able to find rocks with moss.

If nothing is growing where you live, buy small houseplants in the dime store or at a greenhouse. Get different kinds of plants that look nice together, but be sure they require the same growing conditions. You wouldn't put a fern with a cactus, for instance, because one needs lots of moisture and the other hardly any. The number of plants you need depends on the size of the container.

You can also use holly sprigs, although they won't grow without roots. And you'll need a lint-free cloth or paper towels.

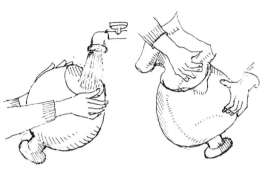

Assembling the Terrarium

Wash the container inside and out and dry it with the paper towels or lint-free cloth.

Mix the gravel with a little charcoal and pour a layer of it into the container, about 1 inch deep.

Then add some soil, mixed with a little more charcoal. Pour the soil into the container to a depth of 1 inch or so—more if the container is deep. In an aquarium, build the soil high in some places and make it shallow in others.

Make a little well in the soil for each plant. If you are using holly and ivy, make wells only for the ivy plants and leave spaces between them for the holly. Set the plants gently in the wells. Start with the large plants, then arrange the small ones around them. Don't crowd them. Pat soil

around the roots. Slowly add just enough water to dampen the soil.

If you want the terrarium to look more Christmasy, add sprigs of holly, mistletoe, or evergreens, pushing the cut ends into the soil.

The lid should be kept on loosely so that air can circulate. Once the terrarium is arranged, it requires very little care. Check the soil once or twice a week and make sure it's just moist. If it's too dry, add a little water. If it's soggy, leave the lid off for a few hours, until it feels right.

Pinch off the tops of the plants as they send up new leaves. This keeps them from getting too tall, and it will make them full and bushy. It won't hurt them at all.

If you are giving a terrarium as a gift, make up a little card to go with it with instructions for its care.

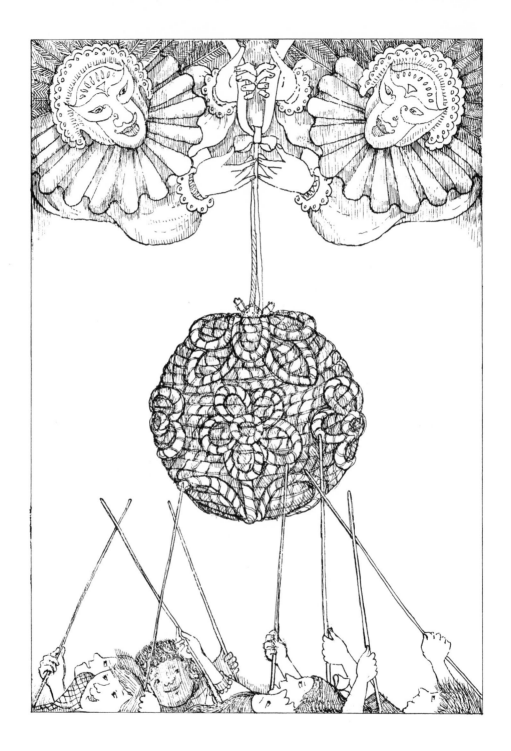

DECEMBER 16 / POSADAS AND PIÑATAS

In Mexico, the observance of Christmas begins on December 16 with Las Posadas (which means "inns" or "lodgings" in Spanish) and lasts for nine days, ending on Christmas Eve. Las Posadas is a series of reenactments of the journey of Mary and Joseph from Nazareth to Bethlehem and their attempt to find a place to stay. Mexican families, playing the roles of the travelers, go from house to house, singing traditional songs in which they ask for shelter. The people in the visited houses take the parts of innkeepers and turn the travelers away heartlessly. At the last home they are finally made welcome. After the religious part of the Posadas is over, attention turns to the breaking of the piñata. Each person, blindfolded, takes a turn at hitting the swinging piñata with a stick, until at last someone breaks the elaborately decorated container filled with candies, coins, toys, and other treats.

The custom of making and breaking a piñata—originally a fragile clay pot—began in Italy, spread to Spain, and was brought to Mexico by Spanish explorers about four centuries ago. In recent years the style of the piñatas has changed from plain clay jars to lavishly decorated papier-mâché figures. They can be of any shape—donkeys and birds as well as simple round balls—but the gay tissue-paper decorations are really more important to a successful piñata than the shape. (A fast way to decorate the piñata is to paint it in bright colors with tempera or enamel, but tissue paper is really more attractive.)

The use of papier-mâché—the words mean "chewed paper" in French and it is actually made of torn paper mixed with paste—dates far back into history and may have originated in China. Easily workable when wet, it dries to a hard, brittle material that is ideal for a piñata.

What You Will Need

For the piñata form: 1 or 2 large round heatproof bowls of the same size *or* 1 or 2 clay flowerpots *or* a large balloon, blown up and tied.
For the papier-mâché: shallow pan, such as a pie pan; fork; ½ cup flour, 1 cup cold water; newspapers.
For assembling the piñata: acrylic or tempera paints and brushes *or* tissue paper in one or more colors; glue or paste, ruler, scissors, strong string, tape, small knife (optional); wrapped candies, nuts, coins, small Christmas favors.

Making the Piñata

The piñata shape is made by building up layers of papier-mâché around a form and letting it dry there. If you use bowls or flowerpots as a form—one for each half of the piñata—you can dry them in the oven in a short time. If you use a balloon as a form, it will take a day or two for the piñata to dry.

Turn the bowls or flowerpots upside down on a sheet of newspaper (if you have only one bowl or flowerpot, you'll make the halves one at a time). Or lay the blown-up balloon on a towel to keep it from scooting around.

To make the papier-mâché, tear several large sheets of newspaper in half, then in quarters. Tear the quarters into strips 1 to 2 inches wide.

88

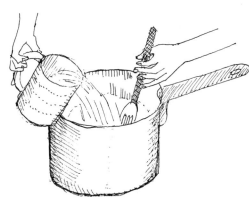

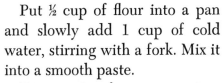

Put ½ cup of flour into a pan and slowly add 1 cup of cold water, stirring with a fork. Mix it into a smooth paste.

Dip a strip of newspaper into the paste, then draw it between your thumb and finger to wipe off the excess paste. Lay the strip across the top of the form. Keep dipping strips and laying them on the form like the spokes of a wheel. Add more strips to fill in the spaces between the spokes. Keep adding strips until the outside surfaces of both halves of the form are covered.

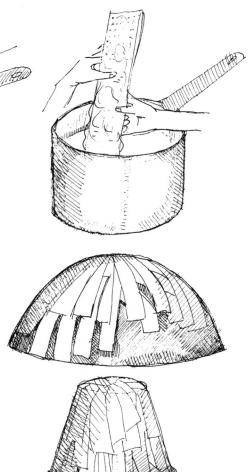

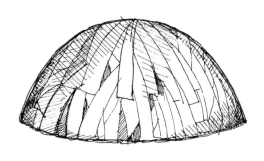

Add a second layer of strips going *around* the form. Then add two more layers, each going in opposite directions. When you are finished, squeeze and mold the papier-mâché with your hands. This smooths the surface and presses out air bubbles and excess moisture.

One end must be open so that you can fill the piñata with goodies. Cut a 2-inch hole through the papier-mâché on one of the halves with the small knife or tear a hole with your fingers at the tied end of the balloon.

If you have used bowls or flowerpots as forms, put them in the oven and turn it on to 200°. In a half hour or so the papier-mâché will have dried somewhat and shrunk so that it can be removed from the form without losing its shape. (If you've made only one half, now make the second half and oven-dry it for the same amount of time.)

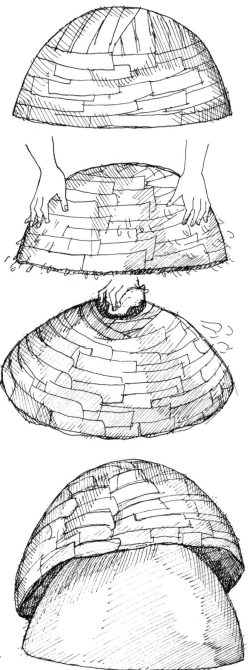

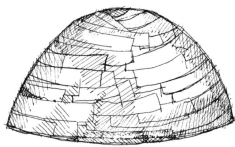

Take the two halves off the forms and put them together with more strips of paper dipped in paste. Make a second layer over the first one. Then put the whole piñata back in the oven for another half hour or so, until it is completely dry.

If you used a balloon for a form, put it in a warm place to dry, but *not* in the oven, because the balloon would burst from the heat and the papier-mâché would collapse.

When the piñata is completely dry, tape a piece of string around it and tie a loop at the top for hanging.

Decorating the Piñata

Paint it in one color, then add wild patterns and flowers. Or cover it with colored tissue paper this way: Cut long strips of tissue paper 6 or 7 inches wide. (For quick cutting, put 3 or 4 sheets together and fold them crosswise once or twice, along the natural fold lines of the packet of paper. Cut the paper in thirds, cutting across the folds.)

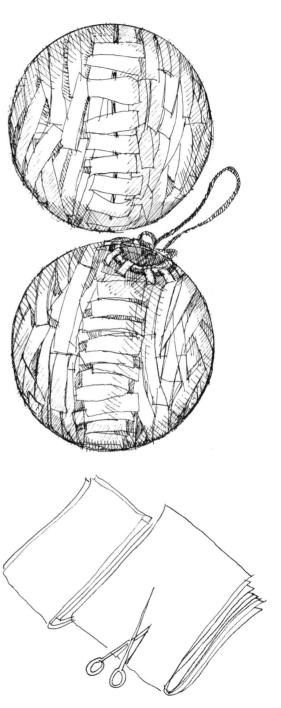

Starting at the open end of the piñata, spread a thin layer of paste or glue in a circle. Twist a strip of tissue paper rather firmly and paste one end of the twisted strip in the center of the circle. Wind the strip around and around the center, twisting as you go, packing each round close to the one before it so that the papier-mâché form is hidden. Paste down the end and continue with another strip. Add round after round of twisted tissue strips until the piñata is completely covered.

Then cut 3-inch-wide strips of tissue paper in a contrasting color. Twist the strips tightly and use them to make designs such as leaves and flowers on the sides of the piñata. You can simply outline the designs by gluing on single twisted strips, or fill in each area of the design with more strips.

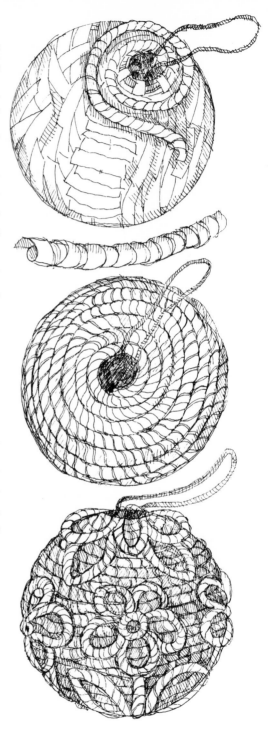

Fill the piñata with enough goodies for everybody and hang it from the ceiling with a strong string just long enough to suspend it above your head. Hang it with the hole near the top. When it's time to break the piñata, give one of the players a broomstick, a baseball bat, or even a rolling pin with which to strike at the piñata. Blindfold the player, turn him around a few times, and set the piñata swinging. Give him plenty of room. Let each person have a few cracks at it until someone breaks the piñata and the treats shower down.

Because a piñata is fun at any time during the holiday season—and, in fact, at any time of the year—it's a nice present to give to someone. Put lots of small items in it, such as wrapped candies and cookies and even inexpensive toys, and attach a note describing how to use it.

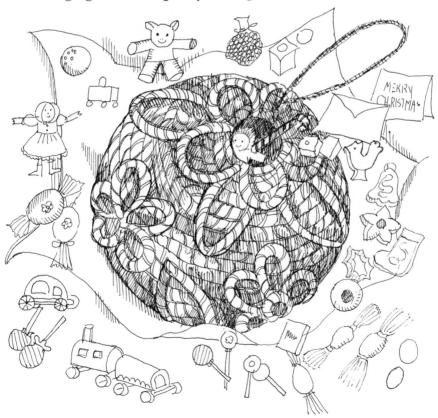

DECEMBER 17 / BREAD-DOUGH CHRISTMAS MANGER

Of all the decorations of Christmas, perhaps none is so well loved—in so many cultures and languages—as the manger, with the Infant Jesus as the central figure. Mary and Joseph, shepherds, animals, kings, and in many places the people of the village, all in miniature, cluster adoringly around him in his little bed of straw.

The first manger scene was the inspiration of St. Francis of Assisi. In 1224, in a cave near a small town in Italy, St. Francis staged a manger scene with real people and animals except for the baby, which was represented by a wax doll. People liked the idea so much that the *presepio,* as it was called, was repeated year after year. People began setting up miniature *presepios* in their homes with small carved figures. Its popularity spread to Spain, where it was called a *nacimiento,* to France as a *crèche,* to Germany as a *Krippe.* And, of course, the idea was carried to both North and South America.

Through history the figures of the manger scenes have been made of many materials, such as wood, clay, ceramic, and straw. Some have been very simple, with just Mary, Joseph, and the Christ Child. Others have been elaborate works of art with dozens and sometimes even hundreds of meticulously fashioned figures.

In Ecuador, the figures of the *nacimiento* are modeled of a clay made of bread dough, painted in bright colors, and finished with a clear varnish.

What You Will Need

Fresh white bread; white glue, liquid detergent, knife, mixing bowl, teaspoon, jar lid or cup, small artist's brush, acrylic or tempera paints, waxed paper, brush-on or spray varnish (optional).

Making the Bread-dough Clay

To make enough bread-dough clay for 3-inch figures of Mary, Joseph, and the tiny Baby Jesus in a manger, mix this recipe: Cut the crusts from 6 slices of bread. Tear the bread into small pieces, then crumble it into a bowl by rubbing the pieces lightly between your hands. Add 6 teaspoonfuls of white glue (wipe the spoon out with your finger each time) and ½ teaspoon of liquid detergent. Mix it all together with your hands. It will be very sticky at first, but the more you squeeze and knead it, the easier it will be to handle. In a short time, the dough will become like clay. If it seems crumbly, add more glue.

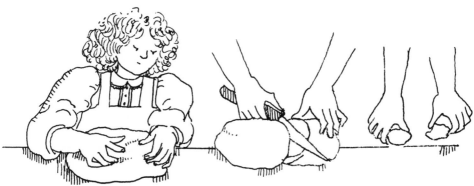

Shape the dough into a roll and divide it in half. Break off a small piece about the size of a walnut from each part. Wrap the large pieces in waxed paper to keep them from drying out.

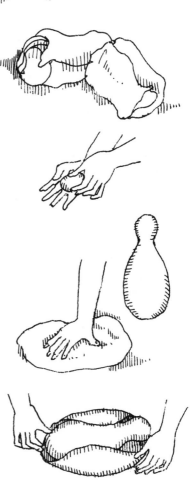

Shaping the Figure of the Baby Jesus

Work one of the small pieces between your fingers and gently shape it into a tiny bowling-pin shape with a body about 1 inch long and a roundish head about ½ inch long.

Shaping the Manger

Flatten the second small piece into an oval pancake a little longer and a little wider than the Baby. Curve the edges up to fit the Baby, but set the manger aside to dry separately.

97

Shaping the Figure of Mary

Break off two pieces the size of peas and roll them out in "worms" to form arms. Roll out a "sausage" for a body, about 3 inches long. Shape a waist about an inch from the top. Flare the bottom out from the waist in a cone shape. Since the Virgin is usually shown with a veil, don't shape a neck. Instead, taper her body from shoulders to top of head without any indentation. Attach the arms with dabs of white glue.

Shaping the Figure of Joseph

Break off two pea-sized pieces to make arms. Roll a sausage for a body, about 3 inches long. Don't shape a waist, but do shape a neck and head. Attach the arms with glue.

Finishing the Figures

Mix a teaspoonful of glue with an equal amount of water in the cup or jar lid and paint each figure with the mixture. This helps to keep the bread dough from cracking as it dries. Set the pieces aside

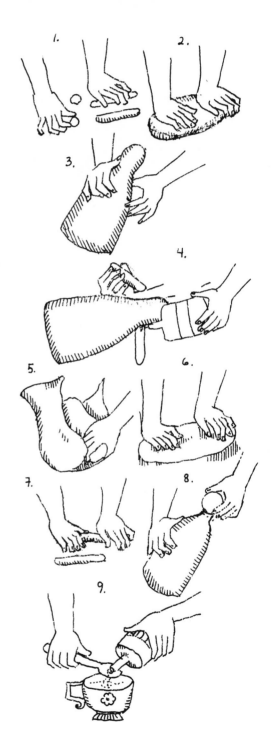

and let them dry thoroughly for about two days, until they are quite hard. Then paint the figures. (You can even leave them plain.) The Virgin Mary is usually dressed in blue, but in South America she is painted in hot colors with flowers on her robe. The Baby's "swaddling clothes" could be white, and his manger painted yellow on the inside, brown on the outside. Give Joseph a black beard and dress him in somber brown or bright South American colors.

This is the most basic manger scene. If you like, you can mix more clay to make shepherds, the Three Kings, and the animals. When you make the animals, use toothpicks in the legs to help support the bodies.

After the paint has dried, it's a good idea to coat each figure with varnish—at least two coats of brush-on varnish or four or more coats of the spray. This protects the pieces and gives them an attractive gloss, but it's not absolutely necessary.

DECEMBER 18 / MAKE-BELIEVE MARZIPAN

Marzipan is a candylike sweet that is especially popular at Christmastime in Germany and Austria. Traditionally it is a rich (and expensive) confection made of sugar and almonds ground to a paste that is then shaped into miniature fruits, vegetables, and other small figures. The town of Lübeck in northern Germany is famous for its realistic marzipan figures.

Make-believe marzipan costs much less to make than the almond-paste kind, but the tiny things you make with it are entirely edible.

What You Will Need

Saucepan, knife (optional), medium-sized mixing bowl, fork, mixing spoon, waxed paper, small cup, small artist's brush, and—

1 very small potato	*or*
1 1-pound box powdered sugar	⅓ cup crushed cookie crumbs
salt	and ½ teaspoon vanilla
⅓ cup ground almonds and ½	flavoring
teaspoon almond flavoring	food colors

Making the Marzipan

Wash the potato and put it in the saucepan with enough lightly salted water to cover it. Cover the pan. Boil the potato gently for about 20 to 30 minutes, until you can stab it easily with the fork.

Run cold water over the potato until it is cool enough for you to peel off the skin with your fingers or the knife.

Mash it in the mixing bowl with the fork.

Add the powdered sugar, a little at a time. The potato will gradually dissolve the sugar and blend with it to form a thick, creamy paste, like frosting. Exactly how much sugar you will need to add depends on the size of the potato.

POWDERED SUGAR

For "real" make-believe marzipan, add ground almonds and almond flavoring and stir them in.

Or, for an easier-to-make marzipan, add cookie crumbs and vanilla flavoring and stir them in.

The dough will be like clay. Roll pieces between your palms to make small balls about the size of a quarter, but round. Shape the balls into apples, lemons, carrots, bananas, strawberries, and whatever other fruits and vegetables you can think of. Place the pieces on a sheet of waxed paper.

Put a few drops of water in the cup and add a few drops of food coloring. Use the brush to paint the pieces, combining colors to make them as realistic as possible. When they are dry, store them in a tightly covered container until you eat them or give them away.

DECEMBER 19 / EVERGREENS FOR THE DOOR

A bunch of evergreens hung by the door is an invitation to woodland spirits to take shelter in your home and to bring health and prosperity to your household. That's what the ancient tribes of Europe once believed. Today, it is another cheery symbol of the season and a sign of welcome to friends and visitors.

Although many evergreen door decorations take the form of wreaths, a few simple branches tied together with a bow are an equally effective way of saying "Welcome—and Merry Christmas."

What You Will Need

Evergreen branches (if you trimmed some from the Christmas tree, they will be fine), 2 yards of wide red ribbon, strong string or wire; and some of these: bells, pine cones, strings of cranberries, colored balls, little Christmas figures, toys, small toy musical instruments, tiny gift-wrapped packages, wrapped candies or lollipops.

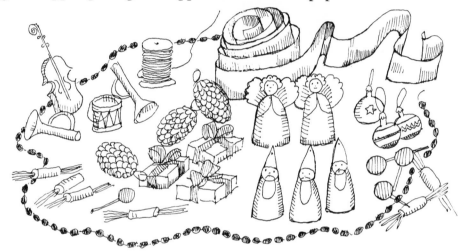

Making the Door Decoration

Tie the branches together with string or wire near the cut ends. It will hold together better if you tie them just below the point where some of the smaller branches join the main branch. Add a loop for hanging.

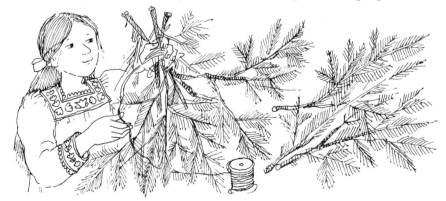

Then tie or wire the small objects and ornaments to the branches. If the wreath is to hang in a protected place, where rain and snow will not fall on it, your choice of ornaments is almost unlimited. But if it will get wet or blown by the wind, you should use only simple, sturdy, weatherproof objects.

Tie a large red bow at the top to cover the cut ends of the branches.

DECEMBER 20 / CROCHETED STAR CHAIN

An interesting Christmas legend with several variations has to do with spiders. In one version, a poor woman, the kindhearted mother of many children, was unhappy because she had nothing with which to trim a Christmas tree for her family. But during the night, the household spiders went from branch to branch of the bare tree, spinning their delicate webs. As a reward for the woman's faith and goodness, the Christ Child caused the webs to turn to pure silver. (Some less imaginative storytellers say it was the light of the sun rising on Christmas morning that caused the dazzling transformation.)

In another telling, it was the spiders who protested to the Christ Child because they were being excluded from the family Christmas celebration (at which the animals were always present) by overzealous housewives who swept them away during the holiday housecleaning. The Christ Child intervened in their behalf, and the spiders repaid the favor by spinning glorious webs for the tree.

Because of these stories, the spider is considered good luck at Christmas in some countries, and spider webs (not usually the real kind, though) trim many trees. You can "spin" a few interesting decorations of your own with yarn and a crochet hook. You may have to practice a bit to acquire the knack of crocheting, but once you learn just two basic steps you can produce a Star Chain.

What You Will Need

Yarn, preferably white, in a medium to heavy weight; crochet hook (use a medium size, such as a G or a 6, with knitting worsted, and a bigger hook with heavier yarn); scissors.

How to Crochet

Begin by making a loop near one end of the yarn. Make the loop by forming two small letter e's next to each other and pulling the second loop up through the first one. Put this loop on the crochet hook and pull the end of the yarn to tighten the slipknot.

Hold the hook in your right hand the way you hold a pencil (if you are right-handed). Pinch the knot between the thumb and middle finger of your left hand and loop the yarn over your index finger. (Reverse these instructions if you are left-handed.) Twist the hook toward you so that the yarn wraps around it, and pull the yarn through the loop on the hook, forming a new loop. The first loop drops off.

When you keep pulling new loops through the old ones, it forms a chain. Practice chaining until you can make the loops fairly even.

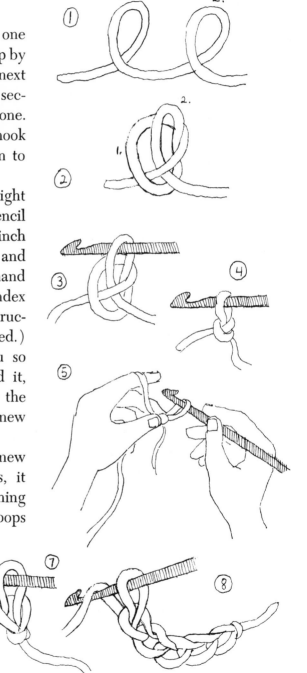

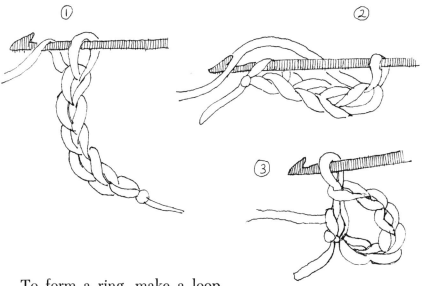

To form a ring, make a loop and chain 6 more loops. Push the hook through the first loop—this makes 2 loops on the hook. Wrap the yarn around the hook and pull it through both loops. This is called a slip stitch and is a way of joining two stitches.

Next try a *single crochet* stitch: With one loop on the hook, push the hook through the center of the ring you just made.

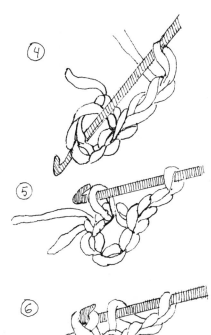

Wrap the yarn around the hook and pull it back through the ring. This makes two loops on the hook. Wrap the yarn around the hook again and pull it through both loops. That completes a single crochet and leaves one loop on the hook.

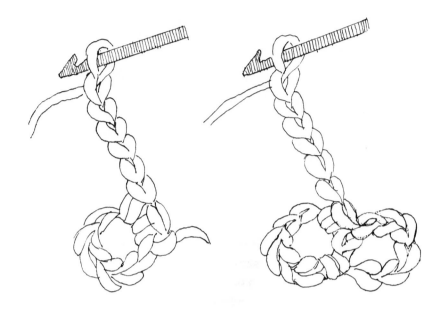

Crocheting a Star Chain

Make a loop for the hook. Chain 6 loops and form a ring with a slip stitch. Make 2 single crochets in the ring. Chain 5 loops. Repeat the "2 single crochets—chain 5 loops" steps four more times. This makes 5 parts of the star around the center ring. Join the last chain loop to the first single crochet with a slip stitch.

Then make a chain 7 inches long. Count back 6 loops from the hook and push the hook through the loop. Form a ring. Work another 5-part star around the ring.

112

Continue making chains and stars until the chain is at least several feet long. Drape it on the branches of your tree. The spiders will be envious. But your friends needn't be—you can give them some as presents.

(To make a single star, without the chain, cut the yarn when you've finished the star, leaving a 6-inch tail, and draw it through the slip stitch. Make a loop with the tail for hanging the star on the tree.)

DECEMBER 21 / "THOMASSING" COOKIES

St. Thomas—one of the twelve Apostles—is not as well known among Christian traditions as St. Nicholas or St. Lucia, but some unusual customs have grown up around his feast day, December 21. At one time, schoolboys in certain parts of Europe chose this day to "bar out the master." The boys arrived at school very early in the morning and made sure that the teacher or schoolmaster could not enter. After some halfhearted pleading and threatening, the teacher gave up and went home and everyone had a holiday.

In other places, the village women went "Thomassing" from house to house, collecting gifts of flour for their Christmas baking.

Instead of an occasion for locking out the teacher, St. Thomas's Day might be an appropriate time for taking her or him a gift—possibly a box of cookies that are both good to eat and nice to hang on the tree.

What You Will Need

Measuring cups and spoons, 1 large mixing bowl, 1 medium-sized mixing bowl, fork, mixing spoon, rolling pin, cookie cutters in Christmas shapes, 2 cookie sheets, waxed paper, pancake turner, wire rack, and—

2½ cups flour
1 teaspoon baking powder
1 teaspoon salt
½ cup soft shortening
¼ cup soft butter or margarine
1 cup sugar

2 eggs
½ teaspoon vanilla
a few tablespoonfuls extra flour
some of these: cinnamon candies,
     silver dragées, candied fruits,
     nuts, raisins

Making the Cookies

Put the flour, baking powder, and salt in the medium-sized bowl and stir them lightly with the fork.

Put the shortening and butter (or margarine) in the large bowl. Add the sugar and "cream" them together by squeezing with your hands until they are completely mixed.

116

Break the eggs into the butter-sugar mixture, and stir them in with the heavy spoon. Add the vanilla.

Pour the flour mixture into the butter-sugar-egg mixture and stir until they are completely mixed.

Divide the dough into four balls, wrap them in waxed paper, and put them in the refrigerator for an hour.

When you are ready to shape the cookies, turn on the oven (or have someone help you do it) and let it heat to 400°. Sprinkle some flour in a circle on the countertop or table where you are working and rub some flour on the rolling pin.

Take one ball of dough from the refrigerator and flatten it with the rolling pin, rolling first one way, then the other, to make a thin circle of dough—about ¼ inch thick.

Cut out the cookies with the cookie cutters. Use a pancake turner to lift each one onto the cookie sheet. Put them close together but not touching.

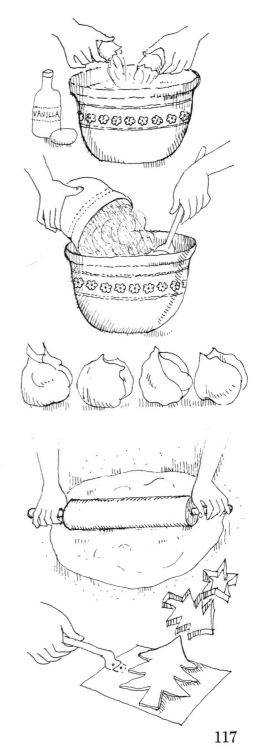

Decorate the unbaked cookies with candies, fruits, or nuts. Or paint them with egg paint (instructions are on page 119) after they are baked.

Bake the cookies for 6 minutes on an upper oven rack. If they are not light brown yet, bake them for 2 more minutes. Remove them with the pancake turner and cool them on the wire rack.

Do the same with the remaining balls of dough in the refrigerator, one by one.

After you have used up the four balls of dough, use the leftover scraps to make wreaths: Roll out long, pencil-thin snakes of dough and tie them loosely at the top. Decorate them with candied fruit before baking or with egg paint after baking.

Egg paint: You'll need 1 egg, a spoon, food colors, a coffee cup, a small artist's brush, and a little saucer or bottle cap for each color. Break the egg carefully and separate the yolk from the white. Put the egg white in a jar, cover it tightly, and put it in the refrigerator for another use. Put the yolk in the cup and stir it. Spoon a little into each saucer. Add a few drops of different-colored food coloring to each. Mix it with the brush. Rinse the brush in *cold* water before you start another color, or have a separate brush for each color. Paint designs on the cookies.

DECEMBER 22 / WASSAIL BOWL

During the Middle Ages, a favorite drink was a hot spiced ale to which eggs, cream, nuts, and roasted apples were sometimes added. The drink was served in a large bowl that was passed around. Before each person drank, he toasted the other drinkers with "Waes hael!" meaning "Be thou well," or "Be in good health."

Henry VIII, king of England in the sixteenth century, is said to have made the drink and the toast a Christmas custom. The bowl had become ornate, and the greeting had changed to "Wassail!" but the ingredients were much the same—and still are.

You can substitute fresh apple cider for the ale and have a hot drink that is welcome on any cold winter day but is especially good to serve to friends at Christmas. So that you can be out having fun with the other Wassailers, mix up a batch ahead of time and keep it in the refrigerator, then heat it up again when you're ready to serve it. Skip the roasted apples if you're in a hurry. This recipe will serve six.

What You Will Need

Pie tin, sharp knife, fork, potholders, large saucepan, mixing spoon, large heatproof bowl, ladle, 6 mugs or cups, 6 spoons, and—

6 very small apples
1 quart apple cider
1 stick whole cinnamon
    (or about ½ teaspoon
    ground cinnamon)

3 whole cloves
some of these: lemon peel or
    slices, orange peel or slices
    (cut *across* the sections),
    almonds, raisins

Making a Wassail Bowl

To roast the apples, turn on the oven (or have someone help you do it) and let it heat to 350°. Wash the apples and cut out the cores and the seeds with the knife. Put the apples on the pie tin and roast them for 30 to 45 minutes, depending on the size and type of apple, until they look ready to burst their skins. Test them with the fork to find out when they are tender, then remove the pie tin with the pot-holders.

Meanwhile, pour the cider into the saucepan and add the cinnamon and cloves. Then put in some of the orange or lemon slices and a handful of nuts and raisins, if you like them. Add a little sugar if you like it sweeter. Stir it with the mixing spoon.

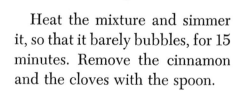

Heat the mixture and simmer it, so that it barely bubbles, for 15 minutes. Remove the cinnamon and the cloves with the spoon.

122

Carefully pour the hot cider into a large bowl. Float the roasted apples in the cider.

To serve it, use a ladle with a handle long enough to reach the bottom of the bowl. Each Wassailer puts an apple in his mug or cup and ladles cider over it. Make sure you dip from the bottom of the bowl, so that each one gets some nuts and raisins. After you've drunk the cider, eat the apples, nuts, and raisins with spoons. Wassail!

DECEMBER 23 / THE BIRDS' TREE

Animals and birds have always been an important part of the celebration of Christmas. St. Francis of Assisi, who founded the religious order of Franciscans in the thirteenth century and is often shown surrounded by birds, believed that animals, too, should be included in Christmas rejoicing because they were present at Christ's birth in the stable.

In many parts of Europe, the animals, too, receive gifts at Christmas, usually in the form of extra portions of food. In the Scandinavian countries, the winter birds are treated to a "bird pole." Traditionally, sheaves of grain from the fall harvest were once set aside. At Christmas the sheaves were tied on high poles for the birds.

Today, a live tree trimmed with food for the birds is an attractive outdoor decoration that also serves an ecological purpose. It is important, though, to maintain the tree throughout the winter, for the birds soon come to depend on it.

If you have a small living tree or bush within sight of your window, it will make a fine Birds' Tree. But if you have none, or if you want to give someone a Birds' Tree as a gift, make a miniature tree. Fill a container such as a flowerpot, large juice can, or bucket with stones, sand, or earth. Arrange a bunch of sturdy branches, either evergreen or bare, in the container.

What You Will Need

Besides the tree itself, use some of these things: string, heavy thread and needle, coarse nylon net saved from fruit or vegetable bags, sharp knife, scissors, cookie cutters, spoon.

And some of these things: seeds, stale bread, nuts, peanut butter, suet; bacon drippings and other fat drippings, hardened in the refrigerator; oranges, apples, popped popcorn, pine cones, cranberries, food coloring.

Decorating the Tree

The two most important items in the diet of winter birds are seeds and fat. Birds also enjoy bread, but you must be careful not to feed them too much of it. Some birds stuff themselves with bread instead of eating foods that provide body heat, and they freeze to death at night. Birds love peanut butter, but it can kill them if it's not mixed with enough seeds (at least 2 parts seeds to 1 part peanut butter). Small amounts of fruit are good for birds, but too much of it can cause dietary problems. Some birds like uncooked suet, but most prefer cooked fat, like fat from frying bacon that has been hardened in the refrig-

erator to a spreadable paste. Ropes of cranberries look pretty on the tree, but the birds probably won't eat them. String the cranberries with small chunks of apple. Try to have a balanced assortment of foods on your tree and be sure to replace things as they are eaten.

When you attach things to the tree, tie some close to the trunk so that the birds that need a stable perch have it while they are feeding. Other birds seem to enjoy swooping in to eat from hanging things.

Here are some things to put on the tree:

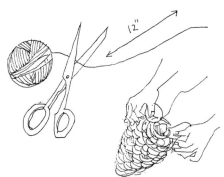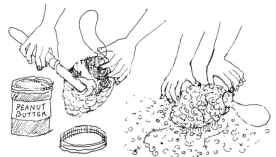

1. Tie a 12-inch piece of string around the upper layers of scales of a pine cone. Spread peanut butter or hardened fat (mixed with seeds) between the scales. Roll the cone in seeds and tie it to a branch by the string.

2. Cut pieces of suet or other uncooked fat into 1-inch cubes.
Thread the large needle with a
6-inch length of heavy thread
and push the needle through the
center of a cube of suet. Pull
some of the thread through the
suet and tie one end around the
suet and the other around a
branch of the tree; do the same
for each cube of suet.

3. Cut an orange in half and
scoop out the pulp with a spoon.
Cut the pulp into slices or chunks
and hang them on the tree with
string.

Punch four holes in one of the
empty half orange rinds, near the
edge. Cut two pieces of string,
each 12 inches long. Thread each
piece through two of the holes.
Tie the four ends together and tie
the hanging basket to a branch.
Fill the rind with seeds or nuts.

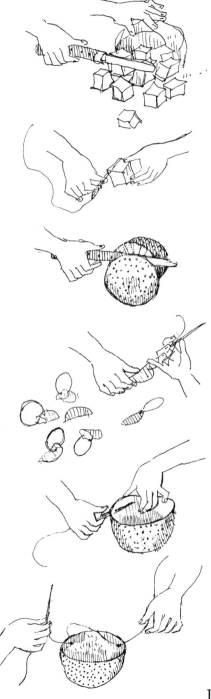

4. Cut 6-inch squares of nylon net from the potato or onion bag. Mix hardened fat with seeds and bread crumbs and put a large spoonful of the mixture in the center of each square. Bring the corners of the square together and tie them with string. Fasten them to branches.

5. Cut slices of stale bread into circles or fancy shapes with cookie cutters. Mix enough food coloring with a large spoonful of hardened fat to give it a bright color. Spread the mixture on one or both sides of the bread. Make a hole near the top of each piece and tie it to the tree with string.

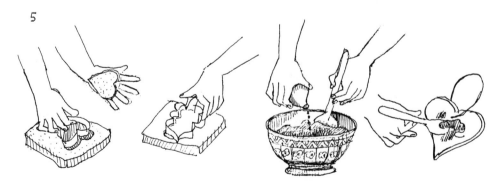

6. Use the needle and heavy-duty thread to string popped popcorn and cranberries and apple cubes. Drape the ropes in swags from branch to branch, then use more string to tie the rope securely to each branch that it crosses.

DECEMBER 24 / CHOCOLATE YULE LOG

Before the birth of Christ, the people of northern Europe believed that the sun was a fiery wheel, and they celebrated with a twelve-day festival when the wheel, bringing light and warmth, started turning toward them again each year. Their ancient word for wheel has come down to the present day as "Yule," and their custom of burning huge logs to brighten the dark days of winter and to scare away evil spirits has become the tradition of the Yule log. In England and other countries in Europe, logs were dragged from forest to home with great ceremony. The burning of the log was a festive occasion, with a piece of last year's log saved to light the new one.

Although not everyone has a fireplace to accommodate a huge Yule log, everyone can enjoy the tradition. In France, one of the treats of the season is the *bûche de Noël*—Christmas log—a cake baked to resemble a log. It's delicious, and there's no reason why any of it must be saved for next year.

What You Will Need

For the cake:

Cookie sheet, aluminum foil, 1 large mixing bowl, 1 small mixing bowl, measuring cups and spoons, table knife, fork, eggbeater or electric mixer, kitchen towel, wire rack, potholders, large serving plate, and—

3 eggs
1 cup sugar
⅓ cup water
1 teaspoon vanilla
1 cup flour

1 teaspoon baking powder
¼ teaspoon salt
a few teaspoons of powdered
　　sugar

For the icing:

4 cups powdered sugar
½ cup cocoa (plain, unsweet-
　　ened)

½ cup soft butter or margarine
¼ cup milk

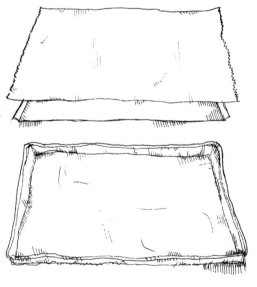

Making the Cake

Cut a piece of aluminum foil about 2 inches longer than the cookie sheet. Fit it on the sheet, smooth it out, and turn up the ends and sides to make a collar all around.

Turn on the oven (or have someone help you do it) and let it heat to 375°.

132

Break the eggs into the small bowl. Beat them hard until they seem thick. Pour them into the large bowl. Wash and dry the small bowl.

Add the regular sugar to the eggs and beat some more.

Add the water and vanilla, beating slowly. Dry the measuring cup so the flour won't stick to it, if the flour isn't already measured.

Put the flour, baking powder, and salt in the small bowl and mix them lightly with a fork.

Add the flour mixture to the egg mixture. Beat slowly just until the batter is fairly smooth.

Pour the batter onto the aluminum foil on the cookie sheet and spread it evenly into the corners. Wash and dry the large mixing bowl and the fork.

Bake the cake for 12 minutes. While it's baking, spread the kitchen towel on the counter or work table. Sprinkle it with powdered sugar.

To see if the cake is done, press the top lightly with your finger. If the surface springs back, it's finished. If your finger leaves a mark, bake the cake for 3 more minutes.

Use the potholders to take the cookie sheet from the oven. Pick up the aluminum foil by the corners and lay the cake upside down on the towel. (The cake will stick to the foil.) Carefully peel away the foil. If you use one hand to hold down the corner of the cake while you peel the foil off that corner with the other hand, the cake won't tear.

Trim off any brown edges. They keep the cake from rolling up properly. You can eat these right now—they're delicious.

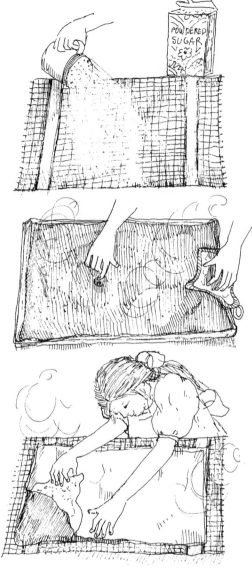

While the cake is still hot, start at one end and roll up the cake and the towel together. Put the cake on the rack and let it cool.

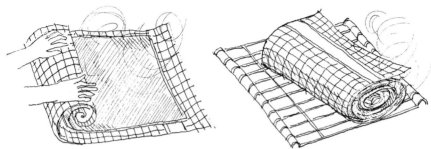

Icing the Cake

Put the powdered sugar in the large mixing bowl and stir it with the fork to break up the lumps. Stir in the cocoa.

Add the butter or margarine and blend well.

Add the milk, a little at a time, until the icing can be spread easily. You might not need all the milk; or you might need a little bit more.

Forming the Yule Log

When the cake is cool, unroll it from the towel. Using the table knife, spread the cake with a thin layer of icing, going all the way to the edges. This should use up about one half to two thirds of the icing. Be sure to save enough for the "bark" on the outside of the log.

135

Roll up the cake with the icing on the inside. Cut off each end of the log at an angle. Put the cake on the serving plate, with the edge of the roll underneath. Use icing to attach the cut-off pieces like stumps of branches on each side of the log.

Spread icing on the log, covering all of it, including the stumps, except the "cut ends" of the log and stumps. Make wavy lines in the icing with the tines of the fork to make the icing look like bark. Add sprigs of evergreens, if you like, to decorate the plate. Keep the log in the refrigerator until it's time for dessert.

Merry Christmas

PAX IN TERRA